QUIRIGUA REPORTS

UNIVERSITY MUSEUM MONOGRAPH 37

QUIRIGUA REPORTS

Robert J. Sharer
General Editor

Wendy Ashmore
Volume Editor

VOLUME I
Papers 1 - 5
Site Map

Published by

THE UNIVERSITY MUSEUM
University of Pennsylvania
Philadelphia
1979

UNIVERSITY MUSEUM MONOGRAPHS

The publication of this volume of Quirigua Papers for the American Section of the University Museum, University of Pennsylvania, is the commencement of a revitalized program of scholarly monograph publication from the Museum.

Titles which will appear in the near future are included in the list of Museum Monographs at back.

Prices are available on request and orders may be placed with the Publication Services Division, The University Museum, University of Pennsylvania, 33rd and Spruce Streets, Philadelphia, PA 19104, U.S.A.

Library of Congress Cataloging in Publication Data

Main entry under title:

Quirigua reports.

    (University Museum Monograph; no. 37)
    Includes bibliographies.
    CONTENTS: v. 1. Papers 1-5, site map.
    1. Quirigua, Guatemala—Collected works. I. Sharer, Robert J. II. Series: Pennsylvania. University. University Museum. University Museum monograph ; no. 37.
F1435.1.Q8Q57   972.81   79-18188

ISBN 0-934718-25-3 (Set)
ISBN 0-934718-26-1 (Volume I)

GENERAL EDITOR'S FOREWORD

This volume marks the start of a series of publications reporting the results of the archaeological research conducted by the Quirigua Project, a cooperative program of the University Museum, University of Pennsylvania and the Instituto de Antropología e Historia of Guatemala. The plan for the publication of the *Quirigua Reports* calls for the first several volumes to appear as soon as possible after the end of the field research in order to present summaries of each season's work, together with other appropriate papers. The present volume includes season summaries for the years 1973-1976. Volume two, now in preparation, will complete the publication of these summaries (1977-1979). Later volumes will present detailed reports of all surveys and excavations, results of laboratory analyses, and conclusions drawn from all aspects of the Project's research.

It should be noted that, over the years, a total of 26 archaeologists and other specialists took an active part in the field investigations of the Quirigua Project. Each of these individuals made important contributions to the successful completion of the fieldwork and to the published results that this volume inaugurates.

Robert J. Sharer
General Editor: Quirigua Reports

The University Museum
University of Pennsylvania
Philadelphia

Funding for the publication of this volume was provided by the American Section Research Fund, endowed by the Coe Foundation; additional funding by Publication Services, University Museum. Proceeds from the sale of this volume will accrue to these funds and will be used to support future publications of the Museum.

ACKNOWLEDGMENTS

The present volume is the first in a series presenting the results of archaeological research conducted by the University Museum of the University of Pennsylvania at the Maya site of Quirigua (see *Quirigua Paper, No. 1*, for the desciption of the publication program). Many agencies and individuals have aided the Project in field and laboratory work, and their contributions are acknowledged specifically in the several papers. Here, however, we should like to note that production of this volume has also been the result of cooperative effort of a number of people.

We are especially grateful to Dr. Maria de J. Ellis, Dr. Erle Leichty, and Martha Roth, all of the Tablet Collection, Near Eastern Section, University Museum, and to Elizabeth M. Christenson, formerly of the American Section, for advice and assistance at all stages of production.

Edward M. Schortman and Patricia A. Urban, assisted by Philip J. Barnes, Patricia A. McBroom and Diana Fox, set the type, and Patricia A. McBroom and Julie C. Benyo helped to assemble the finished pages. All are students at the University of Pennsylvania and a good part of their enthusiastic effort came as donated labor. Final production work was done by the Publications Services Division of the University Museum.

Mrs. Jane Homiller drafted the maps in *Papers 1* and *2*, as well as the site-core map enclosed inside the back cover of the volume. Unless otherwise noted in figure captions, all other illustrations are the work of various Quirigua Project staff members and all are in the possession of the University Museum, University of Pennsylvania.

Above all, we are indebted to Mrs. Francis Boyer and to Mr. Landon T. Clay, Dr. John M. Keshishian and Mr. Alfred G. Zantzinger whose generous support of the Quirigua Project has allowed us to proceed with publication of this volume.

Wendy Ashmore
Volume Editor

Philadelphia

July 1978

TABLE OF CONTENTS

THE QUIRIGUA PROJECT

ORIGINS, OBJECTIVES AND RESEARCH

IN 1973 AND 1974

by

Robert J. Sharer and William R. Coe

INTRODUCTION

Quirigua, a major Maya lowland site located in the vast alluvial floodplain of the lower Motagua valley in eastern Guatemala (see Figure 1), first came to public attention through the visit of Frederick Catherwood in 1840. Since that time the site has been visited and studied by numerous scholars, most of whom have devoted a good part of their attention to the magnificent sculptured monuments. Between 1881 and 1894 Alfred P. Maudslay (1889-1902) recorded the known monuments using photography and molds. Maudslay also instigated the first probes into the ruined structures at Quirigua. In the 20th century, much of the core area of the site (the center of which is now known as the Acropolis) was cleared of debris by successive field projects of the Archaeological Institute of America and the Carnegie Institution of Washington (Hewett 1911, 1912, 1913, 1916; Morley 1913, 1914, 1935). The latter institution sponsored restoration of one structure (1B-1), studies of the hieroglyphic inscriptions (Morley 1937-38), and the resetting of several stelae (Stromsvik 1941). The principal groups of ruins, together with the known monuments, were also set aside as a park during this period, thanks to the land owners, the United Fruit Company. In recent years, the monumental inscriptions have received renewed epigraphic attention (Kelley 1962; Hatch 1975).

Despite this past work, by 1973 very little basic archaeological data was available from Quirigua or the surrounding valley. Apart from the relatively brief time span (ca. 80 years) indicated by the inscriptions, little was known about the time and duration of occupation at the site; no artifactual sequences existed for either Quirigua or the lower Motagua valley. Furthermore, archaeologists knew almost nothing about the construction and function of Quirigua. It is against this background that the Quirigua Project was formed to conduct the first systematic archaeological investigation at Quirigua and within its sustaining valley setting.

ORIGINS OF THE QUIRIGUA PROJECT

For the past forty years the American Section of the University Museum has been engaged in an active program of archaeological research in the Maya area. During this period large-scale field research projects were undertaken at Piedras Negras, Caracol, Chalchuapa, and, most ambitious of all, Tikal. Shorter programs have been conducted at Tayasal and in the Verapaz region of the highlands.

With the research programs at these sites completed, and the publication of the last large programs (Chalchuapa and Tikal) underway, in 1971 the American Section and its curator, William Coe, began to search for another site suitable for a large-scale project. In this search, several criteria were used to assess various sites' potential for future research. A potential site had to be a major center of Classic Maya civilization, located within a relatively unknown region, that held promise for the resolution of significant research problems. Several potential sites, including Quirigua, were visited during this period and eventually seven candidates were selected for serious evaluation. By 1972 Quirigua began to emerge as the most desirable candidate. In addition to fulfilling all the research criteria, Quirigua's accessibility (a new road had just been built to the site), good state of preservation (long protected by the park established by the United Fruit Company), and its well-known status in Guatemala made it especially attractive. Furthermore, since any large-scale archaeological investigation would have to include a program of site consolidation and renovation, Quirigua's location and state of preservation (little or no new masonry would have to be quarried) made it the prime choice.

Accordingly, in late 1972, Coe and Sharer (who had joined the American Section that fall) decided to concentrate upon Quirigua in their effort to create a new research project. In early 1973 both journeyed to Guatemala to present a proposal for a five-year program of archaeological research at Quirigua to the Ministry of Education, its dependency, the Instituto de Antropologia e Historia (IDAEH), and other interested groups, both private and governmental. The precedent provided by the Tikal Project, where the government of Guatemala supported the major consolidation work at the site from 1964 to 1969, was an important consideration in these discussions. Accordingly, the proposal called for the University Museum to fund all archaeological research at Quirigua, while the government of Guatemala was to fund the consolidation and

renovation program.

Encouraged by the positive reception emerging from these discussions, a formal contract between the Ministry of Education and the University Museum was drafted, with the advice of IDAEH. This document, together with our proposal, was submitted for approval through government channels. The contract formally established the Quirigua Project, its responsibilities and its area of operation. The Project was granted permission to conduct all manner of archaeological research within the lower Motagua valley, an area of over two thousand square kilometers extending from Gualan to the Caribbean Coast. Furthermore, it specified the amount of funds that would be expended during each of the Project's five field seasons (1974-1978) by both the University Museum (research) and the Government (consolidation). (See Table 1.) The contract also stipulated that title to the site of Quirigua, situated on land long designated as a park by its owners (formerly the United Fruit Company but recently sold to the Del Monte Corporation), was to be turned over to the government and people of Guatemala.

During this period we learned that Timothy Nowak, a graduate student at Harvard University, was planning to conduct a site reconnaissance and mapping program in the lower Motagua valley. Because of the obvious mutual benefits that would result from a cooperative effort we invited Nowak to join forces with the Quirigua Project. As a result, Nowak's research that began in 1973 (after a pilot study the preceding year) was augmented by funds from the University Museum

Table 1

QUIRIGUA PROJECT CONTRACTED BUDGET

YEAR	GOVERNMENT OF GUATEMALA	UNIVERSITY MUSEUM	TOTAL
1973	3,000	2,900	5,900
1974	13,762	45,025	58,787
1975	12,575	43,025	55,600
1976	17,700	54,350	72,050
1977	17,700	54,350	72,050
1978	15,637	43,737	59,374
1979		20,000	20,000
Totals:	80,374	263,387	343,761

and the assistance of a University of Pennsylvania graduate student. In return for this assistance, Nowak agreed to share all his data with the Project. Furthermore, he would join the Project during its first season (1974) as soon as the contract was validated, and he would continue to be supported by the University Museum through additional research funds and the assistance of another graduate student. Beyond this, Nowak's continued participation and suppport were contingent upon his completion of Ph.D. requirements at Harvard and his seeking of independent research support.

The approval of the contract was formalized by the signatures of the President of Guatemala and his Council of Ministers in December 1973. As a result, the legal basis of the Quirigua Project was established in time for the beginning of its first season, scheduled for January 1974. Unfortunately, upon arriving in Guatemala in January, the Directors were informed that actual payment of the government's share of the funds could not take place until the summer, long after the arrival of the rainy season would halt field operations. As a result, the University Museum had to reluctantly postpone its plans for the major research season at Quirigua in order to maintain the provision of mutual financial support by both parties to the contract. The commencement of research at Quirigua was also set back by delays in the transferral of the park land to the Guatemalan government. However, the archaeological survey of the lower Motagua valley did continue, directed by Nowak, and now conducted under the auspices of the Quirigua Project. In addition the Project opened three test pits (Operations 3B, 3C,

3D) in an area north of Str. 1A-3 that was slated to be the location of the laboratory compound (see below).

The 1974 allotment of government funds was released to the Project in June. However, as expected, the arrival of the rainy season precluded large-scale excavations at that time. Instead, University Museum funds were used to support the continuance of the valley survey and to build Project housing in nearby Los Amates. In the same month the Del Monte Corporation completed its transfer of the 75-acre Quirigua Park to the Republic of Guatemala. Government funds could then be expended for the refurbishing of the site, clearing underbrush and debris, as well as much-needed general maintenance. In the fall of 1974 government funds were used to construct laboratory, storage and service facilities in the park. Three structures were built, designed according to IDAEH specifications so that they could be readily convertible to a permanent museum once the archaeological program was completed.

With all the delays finally ended, the contract provisions fulfilled, and the archaeological survey of the surrounding valley underway, everyone connected with the Quirigua Project eagerly awaited January 1975 for the beginning of the full-scale research program within the site of Quirigua itself. Details of this and subsequent seasons of research will be presented in later numbers of the *Quirigua Reports*. Results of the valley survey and test-pit programs, conducted before and after the creation of the Quirigua Project, will be reviewed later in this paper. But first, the general research objectives of the Quirigua Project will be outlined.

OBJECTIVES OF THE QUIRIGUA PROJECT

The overall research goals of the Quirigua Project have been cast in culture-historical terms, as well as within functional and explanative frameworks, conditioned by the relative dearth of pre-existing archaeological data from the site or the lower Motagua valley generally. The culture-historical objectives were to document a basic chronology of activity at the site, defined in constructional, occupational, ritual and political terms. This was to be done by a combination of deep stratigraphic and lateral excavations within the core of the site, as well as the investigation of a sufficient sample of structures and other activity loci peripheral to the site. The resulting artifactual and architectural sequences would be linked, if possible, to a refined

monumental and inscriptional sequence based upon thorough epigraphic studies. Functional goals were to be pursued by determination of the nature and patterning of structures within the site-core, beginning with the production of a new site map. Similar functional objectives would be sought on the site periphery, with attempts to identify and map outlying groups to determine the nature and distribution of both structures and other activity loci, as well as their relationship to the site-core. The final objective was to test and refine various hypotheses in order to better explain the origins, location, functions and demise of Quirigua. Most of these hypotheses are derived from schemes that have been advanced over the years to "explain" Quirigua's location and functions. The site has most commonly been considered a satellite of the larger center of Copan, located some 50 km to the south (Morley 1920; Kelley 1962). However, others have seen Quirigua as a "break-away" or rebel center that severed its ties with Copan (Proskouriakoff 1973; Hatch 1975).

From an economic perspective, Quirigua has been viewed as an administrative center for a plantation system in the lower Motagua valley, or as a trading center controlling highland-lowland commerce (such as in obsidian) along the Motagua-valley route (Hammond 1972).

RESULTS OF RESEARCH, 1973 AND 1974

As mentioned above, in 1973—before the Quirigua Project was officially formed—the University Museum began its involvement in archaeological research within the lower Motagua valley through its contribution of research funds to the survey conducted by Timothy Nowak. These investigations, which had begun with a pilot study in 1972, were augmented in the summer of 1973 by the participation of a graduate student from the University of Pennsylvania, Douglas Hancock. The survey continued in 1974, then directly under the auspices of the Quirigua Project, by provision of the Project contract. During the summer of 1974 Nowak's work was again assisted by another student from the University of Pennsylvania, Arlen Chase. The following discussion briefly reviews the results of this research, and is based upon a single unpublished report by Nowak (1973), his notes and drawings for Operation 3, his personal communications to the Directors of the Quirigua Project, and the notes and communications provided by Chase (n.d.). It should be noted that, as of this writing, Nowak has yet to provide the Project with copies of his other field notes and his maps as agreed in return for the financial support received from the University Museum.

The archaeological valley survey was aimed at identifying, mapping, and temporally assessing (by surface collections and limited test excavations) prehistoric sites within the lower Motagua valley, an area of ca. 2,125 km². Horizontal control for the survey was maintained by both maps and aerial photographs (at scales from 1:250,000 to 1:50,000). Given the immensity of the area to be covered, and difficulties of transport (although the fruit-company rail system provided access to some areas otherwise inaccessible), Nowak and his two assistants (Hancock and Chase) were forced to conduct a superficial, rather than intensive, reconnaissance of the valley. Only a portion of the area was covered and, in general, the survey was limited to examination of areas along pre-existing roads or rail lines, as well as investigations of possible sites reported by local inhabitants. Vast areas of the valley could not be examined first-hand, and were subject only to aerial-photographic coverage, which was found to be of limited use.

For the purposes of the survey, the lower Motagua valley was sub-divided into four districts (see Figure 1). The first extended from the uppermost limits at Gualan to the area of Los Amates. The second district was defined from Los Amates to Morales. The third extended between Morales and Puerto Barrios. And the final district corresponded to the delta region, from Puerto Barrios to the mouth of the Motagua. As a result of the pilot study, Nowak established a preliminary site typology for the valley. Three provisional "types" were defined: Regional Centers (large, dense and architecturally complex sites), Nucleated Centers (dense, but architecturally non-complex mound groupings), and Dispersed Centers (scattered, architecturally non-complex mounds).

District 2, the largest zone in the valley, with an area of ca. 1,065 km², was surveyed during the 1972 pilot study and during 1973. This area, roughly corresponding to the center of the valley and including Quirigua on its western edge, was found to contain a total of 19 distinct sites, excluding Quirigua. Eight of these were classified as Regional Centers, eight as Nucleated Centers, and three as smaller Dispersed Centers. The Regional Centers appear to be located from 4 to 6 km apart. This preliminary locational pattern allowed Nowak (1973) to estimate that, based upon the area surveyed, perhaps 2 or 3 additional Regional Centers might exist within District 2. The locational data were not sufficient to be able to make similar estimates for the other two classes of sites. District 3 (ca. 650 km²) was also reconnoitered in 1973. Four Regional Centers were located in this area, together with two Nucleated Centers and one site classified as a "large mound grouping." Based upon the area covered in District 3, and the patterning of sites, Nowak estimated that up to 6 additional Regional Centers may exist within the area (Ibid.). District 1 was visited only briefly during 1973, with one Regional Center (ca. 60 structures) being identified. District 4 was not covered in 1973.

The data available for the 1974 valley survey work

are less detailed. No report of the 1974 work, carried out under the Quirigua Project's auspices and with its financial support, has been submitted. According to the information included in several communications, together with notes from the summer work (Chase n.d.), we know that by the end of 1974 a total of 50 sites had been located in the valley, with 21 of these mapped.

In addition to mapping, much of the 1974 season was spent conducting test excavations at several of the Regional Centers in the valley. Nowak supervised three weeks of test pitting at the large site of Playitas (Group B), located in District 2, a few kilometers east of the site of Comanche Farm reported by Stromsvik (1936). Nowak (personal communication, 1974) described finding earth-filled mounds with an overlay of river cobbles, but no cut-stone masonry. He assigned temporal position to the Late Classic, based upon the finding of Copador Polychrome sherds, together with incensario fragments "closely related to San Agustin Acasaguastlan (Magdalene Phase)" (cf. Smith and Kidder 1943). Nowak also noted basic architectural similarities revealed from these tests to those observed at Group A of the Playitas site.

During the summer further testing took place at the sites of Virginia and Group B at Juyama. Virginia is also located in District 2 but is on the northern side of the valley near the foothills of the Sierra de las Minas. Juyama Group B is located on the southern edge of the floodplain, about 15 km east of Quirigua. Excavations at both sites were supervised by Arlen Chase. Three test pits were placed at the Virginia site, two at the bases of two structures, and one in the central plaza. Temporal position was assigned to the Late Classic on the basis of similarities to pottery recovered from Playitas. However, no Copador Polychrome sherds were recovered from Virginia, unlike Playitas (Nowak, personal communication, 1974).

Two test pits were excavated at Juyama. One of these, cut back from a drainage canal that exposed a rich sherd-bearing level, yielded a good sample of Protoclassic and Early Classic ceramics (Usulutan pottery with bulbous mammiform supports, hand-made figurines, "Copan-style candeleros," ring-base vessels and basal-flanged vessels). The other test pit was placed at the base of the principal structure at Group B. Two probable prestructural occupational levels, separated by a sterile alluvial deposit, were revealed (Chase n.d.). Juyama Group A, a large and complex site with quadrangular plaza structures similar to Playitas Group A, is located further south along the valley foothills. It was not tested in 1974.

Other work in 1974 resulted in the location of an apparent obsidian workshop on the first bench of the valley immediately north of Quirigua (Chase n.d.). Another exposure of pottery from a drainage canal was collected at Aztec Farm, located east of Quirigua.

In the fall of 1974 three test pits (Ops. 3B, 3C, 3D) were placed in the park at Quirigua, north of Str. 1A-3 in the area slated to be the site of the laboratory compound. One of these excavations (Op. 3C), supervised by Nowak, revealed an apparent Late Classic midden deposit containing dense concentrations of pottery (Nowak, field notes and personal communication, 1974).

Except for these three test pits, it was understood that the valley survey program would be confined to areas well outside the site of Quirigua. A zone extending roughly 10 km from Quirigua was defined as the area of operation for the Project's Site-Periphery Program, scheduled to begin in 1975 (see *Quirigua Paper, No. 2*, this volume). The valley survey was thereafter given complete responsibility for all areas outside this zone. Unfortunately, lack of funding forced the temporary suspension of the valley survey until 1977.

PUBLICATION PLANS AND CONVENTIONS

Based upon experience in attempting to present the bulk of the archaeological data from both Tikal and Chalchuapa in final report form, the Quirigua Project is committed to a more flexible publication plan. Our goal is to provide our colleagues with the results of the research at Quirigua as rapidly as possible. Accordingly, we plan to collect and issue papers under the present format *(Quirigua Reports)* at periodic intervals during the course of our investigations. The *Quirigua Reports* format is intended to include papers summarizing the

results of each field season's research, together with topical reports representing completed aspects of the research program (such as the excavation of a particular structure, or the epigraphic analysis of a set of monuments). Of course, publication of specialized papers in scholarly journals by members of the Project will also be encouraged. At the close of research at Quirigua, we plan to compile and publish a final report. However, it is hoped that the scope of this final work will emphasize major research results, syntheses and conclusions, since many of the specific data and detailed studies would already have been published in the *Quirigua Reports*.

The terminology and technical standards used by the Quirigua Project in its publications follow those adopted by the Tikal Project (as described in Shook and Coe 1961), with the following modifications instituted at Quirigua:

1. Line drawings of monuments will be published at 1:10, rather than 1:12 as at Tikal.

2. All free-standing sculptured stones at Quirigua are designated monuments, rather than using quasi-functional designations as at Tikal ("altars" and "miscellaneous stones") and previously at Quirigua (see *Quirigua Paper, No. 2*, this volume).

3. Because of the compositional complexity of constructional fills at Quirigua, section drawings will not symbolize these materials; rather fill composition will be described in the text.

4. The term Special Deposit, designated in a running series, has been adopted at Quirigua to describe certain primary contexts sharing the attribute of deliberate interment. At Tikal, these deposits were divided into "burials," "caches," and "problematic deposits." The Quirigua system is designed to avoid functional attributions until final analysis of these deposits is completed.

5. Formal architectural entities at Quirigua will be limited to Structures (generally corresponding to "buildings") and Platforms (generally corresponding to constructions that supported either structures or monuments), eliminating terms such as Terraces and Plazas, except in informal usage (based upon past designations, i.e., the "Great Plaza"). Note that, as at Tikal, both Structures and Platforms will be designated according to their own running series, based upon map grid-square location (e.g., Structure 1A-3 or Platform 1B-4). Buried construction will follow the designation of previously named overlying architecture (e.g., Str. 1A-3-2nd), if clear-cut superimposition is revealed. Buried construction not clearly associated with succeeding architecture will be given a designation within a separate "sub" series (e.g., Platform 1B-Sub.1). The Project's redesignations of previously labeled structures at Quirigua are presented in the following paper (*Quirigua Paper, No. 2*, this volume).

REFERENCES CITED

Chase, A. F.
  n.d.   Unpublished Field Notes, Summer 1974.

Hammond, N.
  1972   Obsidian Trade Routes in the Mayan Area. Science 178: 1092-1093.

Hatch, M.
  1975   A Study of Hieroglyphic Texts at the Classic Maya Site of Quirigua, Guatemala. Ph.D. dissertation, Department of Anthropology, University of California, Berkeley.

Hewett, E. L.
  1911   Two Seasons' Work in Guatemala. Bulletin of the Archaeological Institute of America 2: 117-134.

  1912   The Excavations at Quirigua in 1912. Bulletin of the Archaeological Institute of America 3: 163-171.

  1913   The Excavations at Quirigua, Guatemala, by the School of American Archaeology. Proceedings of the XVIII International Congress of Americanists, London, 1912, Part 2. Pp. 241-248. London: Harrison and Sons.

  1916   Latest Work of the School of American Archaeology at Quirigua. In Holmes Anniversary Volume Anthropological Essays. F.W. Hodge, ed. Pp. 157-162. Washington.

Kelley, D. H.
  1962   Glyphic Evidence for a Dynastic Sequence at Quirigua, Guatemala. American Antiquity 27: 323-335.

Maudslay, A. P.
  1889-1902   Archaeology. Biologia Centrali-Americana. 5 vols. London:Porter.

Morley, S. G.
  1913   Excavations at Quirigua, Guatemala. National Geographic Magazine 24: 339-361.

  1914   Prehistoric Quirigua: The Unfinished City. El Palacio 1 (3): 1-3.

  1920   The Inscriptions at Copan. Carnegie Institution of Washington, Publication 219, Washington, D.C.

  1935   Guide Book to the Ruins of Quirigua. Carnegie Institution of Washington, Supplementary Publication 16, Washington, D.C.

  1937-38   Inscriptions of Peten. 5 vols. Carnegie Institution of Washington, Publication 437, Washington, D.C.

Nowak T. R.
  1973   The Lower Motagua Valley Survey Project: First Preliminary Report. Manuscript, American Section, University Museum, University of Pennsylvania.

Proskouriakoff, T.
  1973   The Hand-grasping-fish and Associated Glyphs on Classic Maya Monuments. In Mesoamerican Writing Systems, A Conference at Dumbarton Oaks. E. P. Benson, ed. Pp. 165-173. Washington.

Shook, E. M. and W. R. Coe
  1961   Tikal: Numeration, Terminology, and Objectives. Tikal Reports No. 5. Philadelphia: University Museum.

Smith, A. L. and A. V. Kidder
  1943   Explorations in the Motagua Valley, Guatemala. Carnegie Institution of Washington, Publication 546, Contribution 41, Washington, D. C.

Stromsvik, G.
  1936   The Ruins on the "Comanche Farm" in the Motagua Valley. Maya Research 3: 107-109.

  1941   Substela Caches and Stela Foundations at Copan and Quirigua. Carnegie Institution of Washington, Publication 528, Contribution 37, Washington, D.C.

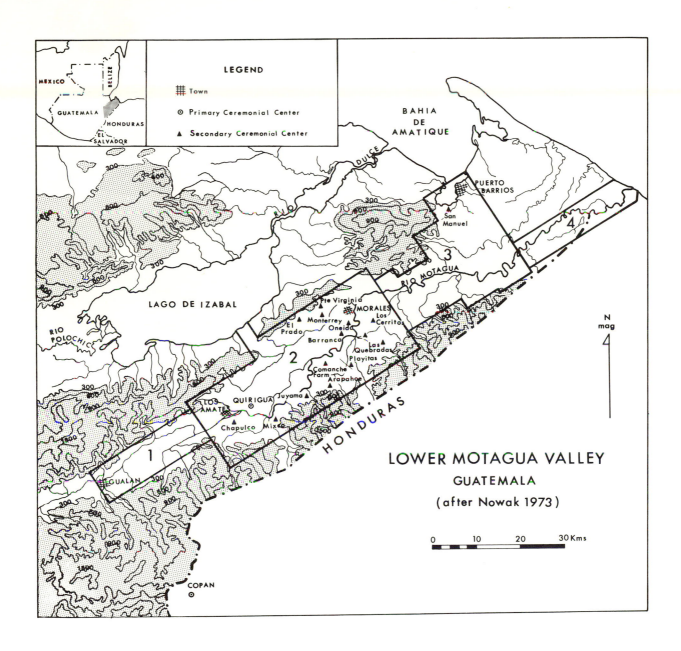

Figure 1. Map of the Lower Motagua Valley showing
Nowak's (1973) survey districts and data from 1973 and 1974.

a

b

Figure 2. Quirigua and its setting.
    a.   View from Group A, looking southeast, with site-core of Quirigua in distance at left.
    b.   Aerial view of floodplain and Quirigua site-core from the southeast, with Motagua River in foreground.

a

b

Figure 3. Project Laboratory and Quirigua Park.
  a. Quirigua Project laboratory compound at north end of Quirigua Park.
  b. Aerial view of Quirigua Park (site-core) looking south along the Great Plaza to the Acropolis. Monument 5 is
      visible in foreground.

THE QUIRIGUA PROJECT

1975 SEASON

by
William R. Coe and Robert J. Sharer

INTRODUCTION

From mid-January to the end of April, and on a very reduced scale into May, the Project carried out fieldwork at a pace made especially intense by having to compensate the loss of large-scale operations in 1974. Within a matter of days the basis for a grid system was laid out at Quirigua, excavation of Structure 1A-3 started, and plane-table and alidade mapping of the site begun. In a short time excavations were underway on Str. 1A-2, Str. 1B-8 and the area bounding Zoomorphs O and P and their altars. Structures bounding the Great Plaza were under heavy growth, requiring brushing, and this work was carried into the Acropolis or what Morley had called the "Temple Plaza." Here heavy excavations and debris removal began by late February. A maximum of some 60 workmen was employed. Among them was a group of Tikal-trained men, the balance being locals; their foreman was Sr. Enrique Monterroso, a person with over a decade of prior experience in this capacity at Tikal and in day-to-day charge there of the huge program of architectural consolidation. The major drawbacks of the season were (1) weather, with irksome rains well into February and truly enervating heat and humidity by April, and (2) inflation, a matter particularly affecting the cost of labor, and one that forced the season to be closed somewhat prematurely.

The following persons composed the staff: William Coe, Robert Sharer, David and Rebecca Sedat, Mary Bullard, Wendy Ashmore, Melvin Strieb, and Robert Hill. Carlos Rudy Larios V. served as Technical Advisor on the part of the Instituto de Antropologia e Historia. Ann Coe and Aura Ortiz periodically aided in the preparation and recording of various monuments.

Costs of staff travel, maintenance and labor for research were borne by the University Museum (Francis Boyer Museum Fund), the National Geographic Society, and the Ford Foundation. Reciprocally, the Ministry of Public Education of the Government of Guatemala funded all work and materials devoted to improvement of the site. The Project also received gratefully substantial donations from the Ministry of National Defense and from the Tikal Association: for this we are especially indebted to the Vice-Minister, General Juventino Gomez Recinos, and to Sra. Laura Recinos de García Prendes. A major contribution was made by BANDEGUA (Del Monte Corporation) in the form of trucks, earth-moving equipment and operators, without which progress in the Acropolis would have been very slow indeed. To Mr. B. Edward Taylor, Mr. Jim Lewis and Ing. Marcantonio Contreras of the company we extend our thanks for this aid, the monetary value of which was truly great. We are also appreciative of the geological advice from John B. Dunlap, Jr. and from Drs. Fred Barnard and Donald McKenzie, the latter two at the request of Mr. Joseph Borgatti, president of EXMIBAL, a subsidiary of the International Nickel Company of Canada. Ing. Antonio García Prendes provided generous and vital assistance in matters involving difficult engineering.

RESULTS OF RESEARCH, 1975

The 1975 investigations were topically divided into mapping, site-core excavation and architectural recording, monument recording, site-periphery reconnaissance and settlement studies, and laboratory processing and analysis.

SITE-MAPPING PROGRAM

In 1975 work was begun toward production of an entirely new 1:2000 plan, with 1-m contour intervals, of epicentral Quirigua—that is, the site-core or what Morley referred to as the Main Group. An up-to-date plan is required by a host of errors (often minor) and omissions in extant ones. The most complete version available is that provided by Morley (1937-38: V, Pl. 214). Apart from misorienting certain monuments this omits the ballcourt reported upon by Stromsvik (1952). The latter repeats the plan of what is designated as the Acropolis (incorporating Morley's "Temple Plaza") and shows the ballcourt situated between the north extensions of the Acropolis. In our mapping we attempted to reconstruct in mound form those edifices exposed by Maudslay, Hewett and Morley, so as to avoid a mixed planar picture of the site. (A revised map, based on Morley's version, is seen in Figure 1.)

Procedurally, the first step was to fix a primary bench mark in the cement floor of the laboratory. This was established as vertically 70 meters, based on a proximate 70-m contour delineated on the 1:50,000 Cartografia sheet for this locale. All mapping (and excavation) is now done with reference to this elevation. Following the example of Tikal (Carr and Hazard 1961), a magnetically oriented grid of 500-m squares has been imposed on the map. The system of designation of the squares is infinitely expandable. One purpose here has been an orderly method of referencing and locating structural entities. In the past a most peculiar approach prevailed, wherein a single series of Roman numerals was applied to "Substructures"—interspersed by a "Pyramid" and various "Terraces"—with a separate series of Arabic numbers for features termed "Temples" (that is, masonry "buildings" or "superstructures"), which contrasted with "substructures" that probably did not support buildings. The ballcourt was simply labeled as such. All in all, this is a good example of a perennial problem in nomenclature, a problem best handled by generous and inconclusive application of the designations "Structure" and "Platform". This leads us to the redesignations

presented in Table 1 (compare Figure 1).

As to outlying "groups" dealt with by Morley as parts of a total Quirigua site, these have been revisited on a number of occasions; comments on them are given in a later section (see Site-Periphery Program).

Table 1

STRUCTURE DESIGNATION

EQUIVALENCES

OLD		NEW	
Substructure	I	Structure	1A-1
"	II	"	1A-2
"	III	"	1A-3
"	IV	"	1A-4
"	V	"	1A-5
"	VI	"	1A-6
"	VII	"	1A-7
"	VIII	"	1A-8
"	IX	"	1A-9
"	X	"	1A-10
Pyramid	XI	"	1A-11
Terrace	XII	—	—
"	XIII	—	—
"	XIV	—	—
Substructure	XV	Structure	1B-14
"	XVI	"	1B-15
"	XVII	"	1B-16
"	XVIII	"	1B-8
"	XIX	"	1B-10
"	XX	"	1B-11
"	XXI	"	1B-12
"	XXII	"	1B-13
"	XXIII	"	1B-9
Temple	1	"	1B-1
"	2	"	1B-2
"	3	"	1B-3
"	4	"	1B-4
"	5	"	1B-5
"	6	"	1B-6
Ballcourt		"	1B-7

SITE-CORE PROGRAM

Our main research objectives were exploratory during the first season, in order to achieve a fairly comprehensive view of constructional stratigraphy and composition, physical articulations, and variations in structural design. Mindful of the development of the site for the visitor, we were attracted to certain obvious features.

STRUCTURE 1A-3
(formerly Substructure III)

With its long axis set east-west, this massive and high feature dominates the north end of the half-kilometer-long Great Plaza and forms the visible backdrop for four of the somewhat oddly arranged northernmost monuments. No prior excavation had been done in this structure, and its principal recorded characteristic (Morley 1937-38: IV, 180) was the apparent lack of cut-stone masonry. Optimistic that this was an accident of decay and mound-formation, our work (as Operation 2) began at the estimated center of the south face, its presumed front. A basal trench here developed into a tunnel, but was soon halted due to the weakness of the fill encountered. Above and on the same line a trench was dug north across the structure and a second parallel trench was made some meters west of the eastern extremity of the structure. Additional narrow trenching exposed features providing the basal outline of the structure, and various superficial probes about the summit provided clues as to the balance of its plan.

What developed in this work was a truly complex entity comprising a presumably original Structure 1A-3-2nd, whose masonry, except that on the north, was almost totally removed in preparation for superimposing a new structure (1A-3-1st) over the whole. Progress on building the latter was halted permanently at about the half-way point; using huge quantities of fill, workers had managed to inter only the north face and central upper portions of the old structure before the project was abandoned.

In brief, 1A-3-2nd had consisted of an 82.5-m-long, 20-m-wide and 7-m-high, steeply pitched substructure featuring along its sides and rear a low basal molding and a massive, continuous second molding above that, rising to the summit. The aproned terraces carried shortly around the southeast and southwest corners where they were terminated at the extremities of a 63-m-long inset stairway. The summit was occupied by a 3-m-wide platform running its entire length, probably with short south extensions at the ends to match the very broad U form of the structure as a whole. The tops of terraces were floored by a crushed rhyolite "plaster." Facing masonry throughout was a mix of marble and rhyolite finely cut small blocks set in a dense mud mortar. The fill had been staged in vertical and horizontal units and consisted of immense amounts of riverine muds and silts as matrix for probably an equal volume of rubble, which comprised seemingly every conceivable variety of sandstone, mudstone, and schistose material, as well as marble and rhyolite and occasional waterworn river stones.

Demolition destroyed the entire stairway except the basal riser which survives one to four courses high (likely its original maximum). The stairway appears to have been pried out block by block rather than stripped away via a deep top-to-bottom excavation. The north face was expanded by marked construction units some 16 m to the north in line with the ends of the old structure, concealing its apron terrace. Centrally, a low rhyolite-faced platform (ca. 30 x 12 m) was built or at least begun; but laterally, to both the east and west, work was suspended at a point where a fill of almost pure river cobbles was being utilized. The north face and sides of this massive addition, designated as 1A-3-1st, were never formally walled; the faces we found were rough retaining walls sealing interior fill units. Moreover, the stairway of 1A-3-1st, presuming it was to have been south-oriented like its demolished predecessor, was apparently never begun.

A thick layer of undisturbed riverine silt overlapped and "sealed" the basal remains of the stairway of 1A-3-2nd and the adjacent terraces. What appeared to be post-demolition wash from the stripped south slope of 1A-3-2nd was also found to drift out onto the old river-stone plaza. Here, the wash admixed with the disintegrated crushed rhyolite surfacing of the plaza, all overlain by the silt. These various features appear to preclude modern robbery of 1A-3-2nd. Similarly this silt, which had accumulated against the base of the expansion known as 1A-3-1st, sealed nothing that could be treated as finished masonry. Unexplained, however, was the need to destroy so much of 1A-3-2nd unless the scheduled replacement of its stairway was to duplicate the original position and pitch, changing only the masonry. The latter might have been planned as large sandstone blocks, for we suspect that such was favored in late times at the site.

Axial trenching at the front of the structure and at plaza level was carried 14 m south, intersecting the far west edge of a previously unknown platform surrounding Stela D (now Monument 4; see below). This clearly had been anciently disturbed, for the naturally deposited silt overlay, not only a demolition line across the surface of the platform, but large blocks of seemingly dislodged sandstone masonry resting on disintegrated plaza flooring and outwash from 1A-3 alongside the platform. Oddly the basal masonry along the west side was rhyolite; a single course of sandstone blocks probably formed the visible perimeter of the platform. However, our trench disclosed an insufficient number of such blocks to restore this side of the platform.

A 2x4-m test pit was dug to the west at a right angle to the central trench. This work disclosed the by-now-familiar .6-m-thick silt layer overlying the formal plaza. The upper limit of the plaza consisted of a one-stone-thick layer of flat river rocks that carried bits of disintegrated granulated rhyolite surfacing; the same layer of cobbles abutted both the stela platform and the surviving first step of Str. 1A-3-2nd. Directly beneath this layer and separated from it by some 10 cm of packed earth and mud was a 1.6-m-thick fill with clear "pause lines," of pure rounded cobbles interspersed by dark mud. This plaza foundation overlay what appeared to be sterile silt. Attempts to deepen the cut at this point were thwarted by the high watertable.

In the course of this work the possibility of a monument having been removed east of Stela D was tested. We found no evidence of this, a result that makes us ponder all the more the asymmetrical arrangement of monuments along the south side of Str. 1A-3 (see Figure 1).

The various related excavations centering on this structure brought to our attention, early in the season, certain marked complexities of Quirigua construction. Since most fills, as just seen, were devoid of sherd material (let alone burials and other special deposits), a problem of ceramic dating of construction arose. Conceivably materials and methods of installation used in building underwent sequent and reconstructable changes. At the same time, one had to ponder the cost of constructional material here, with sedimentary sandstones brought from 3.5 km north of the site, marble from a much greater distance (some 20 km), rhyolite from a totally unknown volcanic source, and metamorphic serpentines from perhaps as much as 10 km away, to say nothing of the staggering volume of muds and cobbles from the river itself. Even granting that some of the raw materials were possibly collected from natural taluses, one must still add to these collection costs the labor of dressing marble and rhyolite. To our minds, most extravagant was the presence in fill of chunks of

marble and rhyolite, probably too large to have been mason's detritus; weighty pieces were apparently brought to the site along with more easily available sandstones simply as volume-making fill. Str. 1A-3 also presented the enigma of construction work being permanently halted, a major edifice being left in shambles, and of course the question of cause and probable links to abandonment of the site.

In our opinion, excavations should be renewed here as soon as feasible. First, there remains the possibility of a still earlier structure beneath 1A-3-2nd; further axial tunneling is dangerous and the approach should be a trenching operation. Importantly the thick cobble plaza has yet to be sectioned beneath the structure; it must end at some point there since no trace of it occurred in our probes along the north side of the structure. Furthermore, the spatially associated monuments here should be physically interlinked and stratigraphically tied to the structure. Finally, some method should be devised to penetrate significantly the silt beneath the cobblestone foundation of the plaza, although we see little reason to doubt a natural origin for it.

STRUCTURE 1A-2
(formerly Substructure II)

Excavation of this structure was completed during the 1975 season. The report of this work (Op. 5) will be presented in a future paper in this series.

THE ACROPOLIS

Although the Acropolis has been long published in plan, its awesome size and intricate conformation became apparent to us only after the high underbrush covering it was cleared early in the season. Simultaneously, the extent of its deterioration became depressingly apparent, as did the enormous amounts of old excavation "spoil" throughout the area of the Acropolis Plaza (Morley's "Temple Plaza"). As had long been known, the five buildings exposed from 1894-1919 by Maudslay, then Hewett, Morris and finally Morley had seriously deteriorated and rooms once cleared had become half-obscured with fresh debris.

A major multi-season program would be required here not only to reclear, to sort and stockpile the many tons of discarded masonry, but to analyze the growth and composition of this huge amalgam of buildings and platforms. This is an obvious focus for analytic excavation and public development. But, at the outset, two major drawbacks existed: how to remove the staggering quantities of material choking the plaza area and how to contend with the miserable records of past excavation—records that Ricketson's 1933 field notes realistically tag as "scientifically useless."

Our initial step, that of digging out the collapsed interiors of buildings, only exacerbated the first problem, for after stockpiling all recoverable masonry nearby, the huge balance of dirt had to be dumped into the plaza area. The obvious exit for all debris was from the opening on the northeast side of the plaza. Such salvage, let alone original excavation, would have been practically precluded had not trucks and a front-end loader been made available. This was a sensitive operation, one spread over weeks, that required hand separation of plain and carved masonry, piling of the latter close to its obvious or likely structural source and removal of the plain material from the plaza out to the east where it was hand-stacked in individual spots marked to correspond to known or probable original structural proveniences. Thousands of cubic meters of residue—dirt and debris—were trucked beyond the Acropolis and piled for eventual use, for instance, in backfilling trenches and for repair work at a later time. As the season closed, the effect of men and machinery was a plaza 90% free of old debris as well as that produced by our fresh excavations.

Determination of the original condition of the mounds and "inter-mound" areas was a serious problem because of the virtual lack of records from the past excavations. Except for work by Ricketson and possibly at one point Hewett, the former excavations were conducted at a late, shallow level. Fortunately, the huge bulk of constructional buildup was untouched by the early excavators. What have been lost are the sequence of collapse (which made the mounds) and the detailing on roofing, capstones and vaulting. The evidence of secondary features between structures was on occasion nearly obliterated. Furthermore, intricate facade ornamentation in stone was recovered in the past in a totally uncontrolled fashion, then scattered, or at best placed in common piles. We also find ourselves having to contend with post-excavational collapses, as well as illegal digging and even robbery of once-recorded sculpted stones. A modern complication is the great central sandstone stairway leading down to the Ballcourt Plaza and Zoomorphs O and P (Monuments 15 and 16). As badly tumbled as its east extension, this stairway appears to have been in part roughly reset by the Instituto Guatemalteco de Turismo (INGUAT) sometime about 1970. While at times we felt the Acropolis perhaps hopelessly brutalized, it is archaeologically salvageable.

Excavation began here in 1975 (as Op. 6) by probing and recording dozens of constructional joints between floors, walls and steps that had come to light as the result of Morley's excavations and subsequent weathering about and between Strs. 1B-3 and 1B-4 along the west side of the Acropolis Plaza. Similarly around Str. 1B-1 to the south as well as nearby Str. 1B-2, a considerable number of sequent features were exposed after our clearing. A 4.6-m-deep test pit dug by Ricketson in 1933 in the plaza near the northeast corner of Str. 1B-2 was re-excavated. As a result, it became rapidly clear that both the plaza and flanking entities had had a complex growth involving superimposition, demolition, overlap and probably intrusion as well. Equally evident to us was the great variation in masonry materials and forms among the entities constituting the final version of the Acropolis. Indeed it seemed probable that the vast, possibly incomplete platforms forming the north part of the Acropolis were late additions made of massive sandstone blocks and a fill of river cobbles.

Two trenches were laid out, one (Op. 6F) east-west, to be cut from the central court west to the western base of the Acropolis, the second (Ops. 6A and 6I), north-south, to be run from Str. 1B-5 through the Acropolis Plaza, Str. 1B-1 and terminating at the south base of the Acropolis. Both trenches could eventually connect in the Acropolis Plaza, and an eastward extension would intersect Str. 1B-6. With this as strategy, considerable progress was made during the 1975 season.

Excavations down in the Acropolis Plaza verified four distinct stages of growth. The earliest was based on apparently natural silt which, by its level, should be the same stratum encountered beneath the Great Plaza foundations to the north. The early Acropolis Plaza consisted of a 1.2-m-thick fill, twice floored with a crushed rhyolite plaster. Later a .6-m-thick foundation was installed throughout the plaza and then plastered. In time, a third foundation was laid, again .6 m thick and plaster-surfaced. The final stage of growth comprised a 1.5-m-thick layer of fill capped first by a continuous tightly fitted paving of large, relatively thin "lajas" that was immediately sealed by the familiar rhyolite-based plaster; there are traces of two subsequent refurbishings of this floor. The plaza thus incorporates close to 4 m of vertical growth and the four stages were found both to the west and south to integrate with a most complicated series of terraces and associated stairways, often with secondary additions. Partially dismantled buried buildings were found at plaza level and above and to the sides of the Acropolis Plaza. Various stratified floors and terraces were found covered by thick masses of compacted charcoal, censer fragments and crushed pottery. Major structural rip-outs were also found in both trenches and beneath Str. 1B-5.

From an architectural standpoint, most surprising were two cases of free-standing, non-bearing walls. One runs east-west and abuts a west-oriented range-type building of rhyolite masonry, all deeply buried beneath the relatively late short series of terraces and stairways just north of Str. 1B-1. The second example lies concealed beneath a most intricate series of constructions forming the west upper side of the court and positioned between build-ups culminating in Strs. 1B-3 and 1B-4. This particular free-standing wall originally must have stood somewhat over 4 m high (with a width or thickness of 1.4 m). Made of small facing blocks of yellow sandstone, it likely formed the east wall of a large patio open to the west. How access to the court to the east and below was gained has yet to be found. Most strikingly the uppermost reaches of the west side of the wall were decorated by a row of five mixed rhyolite and sandstone masks, monumentally scaled and in deep relief, that alternate between depictions of *Kinich Ahau* and a serpent with human arms. In each case the mask is supported by a frieze consisting of two concentric ovals flanked by large profile serpent heads. Unhappily only the southernmost mask escaped extensive destruction during relatively late building activity. Lying as they do beneath the extremities of Strs. 1B-3 and 1B-4, the corresponding south and north walls have yet to be probed. To do so will require furthering multiple cross-cutting trenches necessary to document the sharp shifts in orientation of the overlying constructions.

As part of the 1975 excavations in the Acropolis, excavations were carried out about the great zoomorphs and associated altars (Monuments 15, 16, 23, 24) at the north central base of the Acropolis (Op. 4). This work was principally clued to recovering local stratigraphy involving the relationship of the monuments to the Ballcourt Plaza, to a broad low platform or terrace forming a common support for the zoomorphs, and finally to the frontal ballcourt as well as the great red sandstone staircase leading up onto the Acropolis. Although the work was impeded by earlier cache-oriented cuts here (Morris and Stromsvik in 1934), it seems reasonably certain that we are dealing first with basal natural silt, then the formation of plaza foundation of river stones (here about a fourth the thickness of the foundation seen at the north end of the Great Plaza), then the platform, and finally the sandstone Acropolis

stairway. It is mandatory that work in a later season include not only linking the ballcourt to this constructional series, but also following the Ballcourt Plaza and zoomorph terrace south beneath the stairway, relating them to the rapidly emerging sequence of Acropolis events. Particularly intricate will be application of Maya dates of the monuments to the Acropolis, for which we otherwise have only the quite secure date of 9.19.0.0.0 (Str. 1B-1, presumably at or close to its time of construction). The sequential relationship of the zoomorphs to the platform visually sustaining them is still to some degree ambiguous.

While only about two months were given to studies in and about the Acropolis this year, we did end the season with the broad outlines of a markedly tortuous sequence of construction and use—a sequence of three-dimensional complexity exceeding at some points that encountered, say, in Tikal's North Acropolis. But unlike the latter, the Quirigua Acropolis evolved rapidly and that which the trenches have so far revealed appears tightly compressed into perhaps no more than two centuries of Late Classic times. If so, changes in design and masonry and building methods were intriguingly swift.

THE "SOUTH GROUP" AND STRUCTURE 1B-8
(formerly Substructure XVIII)

Excavations in this group were completed during the 1975 season. The report of these investigations (Op. 7) will be presented in a future paper in this series.

MONUMENT RECORDING PROGRAM

After reviewing the extant record of Quirigua sculpture our reluctant conclusion is that we ought to assemble a fresh and comprehensive photographic file on this material, particularly by artificial light. With this as the basic control, inked diagrams in line and stipple could be prepared at a standard scale, as was done for Tikal and elsewhere by others, notably Ian Graham (e.g., Graham 1967). For Quirigua this will be no easy task, faced as we are by the size and, in some cases, the three-dimensionality of the sculptures. Although Annie Hunter's drawings—published with Maudslay's photographs—are admirable products, much can be done to improve on them. Of course, important sculpture was found subsequent to Maudslay's time, but Morley, their principal illustrator, publishes photographs which appear inadequate as records; too often, it has to be admitted, his photographs were poorly taken for his purposes.

There is also the matter, in our minds troublesome, of designating "monuments" at Quirigua. Morley continued Maudslay's alphabetical series, adding new capitalized letters for freshly discovered items. Each letter was prefaced by a descriptive term, and thus we have Altars, Stelae, Zoomorphs, in two cases Altars of Zoomorphs, and finally a lettered Sculpture and an Unsculptured Stela. The term "altar" covers three small "zoomorphic," three-dimensional sculptures as well as three unifacially sculpted flat discs. Yet, huge irregularly shaped flattish stones fronting Zoomorphs O and P are called "altars" but left unlettered, and attached for reference purposes to the zoomorphs. The "Unsculptured Stela" is humbly unlettered possibly because of its plainness, and one might question use of "stela" for what is, in fact, a column. Sculpture W, the last of Morley's series, was rediscovered this season. As Morley guessed, it is a member of an unknown hieroglyphic frieze. Only at issue is its inclusion in a series of non-architectural, free-standing sculptures. Or are we really dealing with "monuments"? The latter term does have the advantage of simplicity and it is open-ended. Hewett (1911) originally employed "Monument" and number, but this system was evidently passed over by Morley and is now forgotten.

Sensitive to the prospect of new monuments being found in the *site* of Quirigua, however defined (a crucial problem in itself), we do believe there is merit in a numbered series of monuments. The progression of numbers in Table 2 follows that of Morley's letters and we suggest "Sculpture W" be dropped.

We, finally, would point out to those colleagues inimicable to such changes the matter of the discerning visitor's understanding. Questions as to what is a zoomorph, an altar and so forth are commonplace at Quirigua, as we discovered, let alone the presumption of a "Zoomorph A" somewhere nearby, in light of a well-labeled Zoomorph B confronting visitors as they

Table 2

MONUMENT DESIGNATION EQUIVALENCES

MORLEY DESIGNATION	PROJECT DESIGNATION	PRESENT LOCATION
Stela A	Monument 1	Quirigua
Zoomorph B	Monument 2	"
Stela C	Monument 3	"
Stela D	Monument 4	"
Stela E	Monument 5	"
Stela F	Monument 6	"
Zoomorph G	Monument 7	"
Stela H	Monument 8	"
Stela I	Monument 9	"
Stela J	Monument 10	"
Stela K	Monument 11	"
Altar L	Monument 12	National Museum, Guatemala
Altar M	Monument 13	Quirigua
Altar N	Monument 14	"
Zoomorph O	Monument 15	"
Zoomorph P	Monument 16	"
Altar Q	Monument 17	"
Altar R	Monument 18	"
Stela S	Monument 19	" (Group B)
Stela T	Monument 20	" (Group A)
Stela U	Monument 21	" (Group A)
Altar V	Monument 22	Peabody Museum, Cambridge
Altar of Zoomorph O	Monument 23	Quirigua
Altar of Zoomorph P	Monument 24	"
Unsculptured Stela	Monument 25	" (Group C)

enter the site-core. And, of course, where is Stela B? While we are reluctant, almost by a matter of training, to advocate change in designations so long in effect, we feel the change is amply justified in this case.

To shift to a more sanguine topic, various barely recorded monuments were documented this year. Notably, the sculptured surfaces of Monuments 23 and 24 were plotted, then photographed, and converted finally, in Philadelphia, to quarter-scale, inked, standardized diagrams. Sculpture that carries over the sides (severe in the case of Monument 24) has been flattened out. These superb sculptures do warrant the maximum accolade given them by Morley. Their texts are under study at this time by Christopher Jones.

The seemingly miniature Monuments 18 and 19 were also recorded. One is badly eroded; the other possesses minute detailing marred by deeply embedded lichens. Scenically they are mirror images. Only provisional drawings are possible until more cleaning is completed and critical photography is done with artificial light.

SITE-PERIPHERY PROGRAM

The balance in research at Quirigua today, not remarkably, depends not only on comprehensive climactic, epicentral investigation, but also on definition of total site or community; the structure, interaction and function of its population; its distribution spatially and in time; and inevitably the basic economics (including subsistence) and socio-political arrangements that provide some if not the whole explanation of the data. As a simple guideline to research, an Acropolis reciprocates with a small residential unit some kilometers north of it, and to overemphasize one would be to obfuscate the understanding of both. Of course, here we are dealing with a simple model that glosses over gradients of social complexity, of architectural magnitude, and of spatial separation.

Interest in the essentially assumed "macro-site" of Quirigua begins by taking into account the outlying "groups" described by Morley as well as the "small structures" investigated by Hewett on the first bench above the north extremity of the alluvial plain of Quirigua. Parenthetically, it is of some historical interest that Hewett, bent seemingly on securing dramatic material at Quirigua proper for a precolumbian exhibition in San Diego in 1915, did in fact excavate at least one probable "house" on the first bench (Hewett 1912: 165-166). This was one of the first instances of active attention being given to such relatively mundane

entities in Maya research. The location of these excavations, however, remains a mystery to us, and in fact the few mounds he dug may have since been destroyed.

Our objectives at this stage are basic and modest: locate, map, surface-sample, and selectively excavate archaeological loci throughout the valley floor immediately adjacent to "Quirigua" (within a 5 km radius of the site-core). This area includes the surrounding floodplain, the first and second benches of the valley north of the site and the zone to the south across the Motagua River where large numbers of mounds are known to exist.

As to remains (domestic or not) along the benches to the north, the evidence is inevitably obscured, if not in fact partly obliterated, by the essentially continuous, relatively recent settlement provided by Los Amates and modern Quirigua. The valley floor has been subject to probably serious modifications, first by banana plantations and now by cattle, let alone their attendant irrigation canals and watering holes. Alluviation, a marked fact here, has totally buried domestic remains of no substantial elevation and has reduced the prominence of more elevated remains. A potential method of discovery here lies in magnetometer survey. Pulse-radar, according to the Museum Applied Science Center for Archaeology (University Museum), could prove an enormously productive alternative in this situation. Another approach, and a feasible one in a later season, would be to bulldoze clean and perhaps deepen the edges of the drainage ditches alongside the 3.5-km access road connecting the site-core and the highway to the northwest. In this manner, an archaeologically definitive sample of potentially extant remains relevant to population could be gained. Additionally, we should try a program of systematically placed cores. And finally, the Project should further follow the lead given by Timothy Nowak by scouring the boundaries of drainage ditches and canals so plentiful in this locale. Such an approach did in fact produce results relevant to Quirigua this season.

The site-periphery survey for Quirigua was initiated in 1975 by Wendy Ashmore. First, the areas of the first bench to the north and west of the site-core were reconnoitered (Op. 8), and observable mounds and their clusters were mapped. Surface collections at such loci were generally sparse but one group of six mounds yielded abundant obsidian debitage. Structures along the first bench were found located close to the low but precipitous drop to the valley floor. All remains are close to present-day water sources (springs or *riachu-*

elos). Mounds here are small, being less than 10 m in any dimension, and form groups of fewer than 10 entities. Time permitted the test-pitting of only one mound on the bench (Op. 8Q), work that yielded a few coarse sherds and some obsidian. With sparse cobble inclusions, fill consisted mainly of tamped earth. The summit had been floored no more than twice, but positive evidence of a building was lacking on the platform. Other disturbed mounds adjacent to the Project's camp in Los Amates show evidence of a nearly pure riverstone fill (Op. 8R). Interestingly enough, today the flat sweeps of the Motagua River fronting Los Amates continue to be "mined" commercially for riverstones for use in construction.

On the valley floor, mounds are distributed singly as well as in clusters of fewer than five. A possible ballcourt occurs northwest of the site-core. Such still observable mounds, alone and grouped, are generally separated by distances on the order of 100 meters. The visibility afforded by recent conversion of former banana land to cattle pasture helps sighting, but, as noted above, alluvial accumulation buries all but the highest precolumbian remains. With this in mind, a mound merely .6 m high was tested (Op. 8P) northwest of the site-core. Accounting for this elevation were slumped masonry walls and benches; the 1-m-high substructure lay .2 m *below* the present ground level. The potentials of the valley were further tested by reconnoitering an old drainage canal running north-south about a kilometer east of the site-core (Op. 8S). Fairly large numbers of surface sherds were collected quite continuously along the roughly 1000 m of embankments inspected.

The extent and intensity of ancient habitation on the valley floor about the epicenter are crucial matters and ones obviously to be pursued in coming seasons. We have speculated that occupation was probably sparse at best over this rich-soil area, as it would have been devoted to intensive agriculture and most particularly to plantations of oil palms and cacao; further, that population was largely along the north valley benches with the result that ancient and modern patterns of settlement are basically alike.

In 1975, the survey reviewed Morley's outlying Groups A, B, and C. In Group A, high on the second bench with a splendid view of the entire valley, it was found that Morley had omitted a long, narrow mound along the west side of the main platform-plaza as well as a probable mound at the end of a possibly natural ridge running north from the main platform. Early Monuments 20 and 21, long toppled and abandoned, were relocated in Group A. (It is planned that these be moved

for safety and study to the site-core.)

As regards Group B, the mounds were found not to be so symmetrically arranged as Morley (1937-38: V, Pl. 215b) shows them. Monument 19 also appears in plan too far south. This incomplete stela strikes us as likely having been reset here as a fragment.

Group C, barely described in the literature (Ibid.: IV, 241), is today visible from the Atlantic Highway and consists of five substantial mounds, four of which occupy a plaza overlooking the Quirigua River. On this plaza, two mounds, each about 15 m by 22 m basally and 3 m high, face each other and are separated by an east-west distance of about 42 m. Midway is set Morley's Unsculptured Stela (Monument 25), a plain cylindrical shaft about 2.75 m long and .46 m in diameter. Two lower mounds lie south of the monument, and, south of these, flat, possibly artificial terracing drops several meters to the river. Set on the crest of a natural rise, the fifth mound of the group is about 120 m north of the plaza. No surface sherds or other artifacts were found in this group.

LABORATORY CLASSIFICATION AND ANALYSIS

In 1975 a field laboratory was established in the Project's compound east of the entrance to the site-core. Under direction of Mary R. Bullard, all artifacts recovered during the season were washed, catalogued, conserved when necessary, and stored. Only pottery was analyzed this season but a variety of technical studies are planned in 1976. Processing covered such materials as some 1580 fragments, nodules, and artifacts of obsidian, 55 groundstone artifacts (largely manos and tripodal metates), 46 lot bags of censer fragments and 161 lot bags of sherds. Obsidian promises to be a major study category and one that is additionally intriguing in light of the hypothesized role of Quirigua in the trade of Ixtepeque material (Hammond 1972: 1093). Pottery censers also impress us by their frequency. The stratigraphically intermediate levels of the Acropolis have yielded abundant deposits of crushed censers of one particular marked form: a shallow, broad "hourglass" receptacle with three medially inclined hollow prongs on the periphery of a heavily scored bowl; a low, rounded cover with handle sits on the prongs. Surface finds of fragmentary censers are also quite common, tending to display vertical flanges with elaborate applique work. Strikingly, we have yet to see flint in any form appear in the day-to-day collections. Pottery figurines too have so far proved to be most rare.

A preliminary study of the 1975 collections of Quirigua ceramics was done by Robert J. Sharer in the last weeks of the season in order to assess the possibilities of chronological change and functional differentiation within the site. To do this, a rough typological classification was made following the procedures of the type-variety-mode method and resulting in the definition of 19 type-variety units organized into six ceramic groups. The sherd sample consisted of (a) material from two test pits within the laboratory compound (Ops. 3C and 3D) and (b) sherds recovered in sequent constructional and occupational units within the south trench in the Acropolis (Op. 6I). These two sources have to date been the most productive, for most excavation lots have been in fills either sterile or nearly so.

In the south trench of the Acropolis (Op. 6I), the pottery from all but the uppermost levels is generally uniform and appears to correspond to a Late Classic period. High frequencies of broken pottery censers presumably result from ritual activity. A shift in content occurs in the upper levels consisting of a reduction in frequency of earlier ceramic groups and the appearance of two new types forming a distinct ceramic group. The meaning of the shift is not known, but, assuming primary context, it is probably a reflection of either a chronological change to the Terminal Classic or even Early Postclassic, or, perhaps, a use-related functional shift indicating a change in behavior patterns. The latter interpretation may have special weight since pottery of the upper levels appears to be domestic in contrast to very common ritual material (censers) in the lower levels. On the other hand, chronological differentiation might be favored inasmuch as the two new types in the upper levels are absent in the lots from the two test pits in the laboratory compound. Some ritual pottery (censers) occurred in

these tests but most material can be considered domestic, including one unslipped type not found in Op. 6I of the Acropolis. These tests furthermore produced the only Preclassic sherds within the site-core of Quirigua. Late Preclassic and Protoclassic sherds are present in disturbed contexts along a drainage ditch a kilometer to the east (Op. 8S; see Site-Periphery Program).

From these initial analyses, it appears that the pottery from Quirigua proper is limited in both time span and diversity. With the exception of the few Preclassic examples noted above, all sherds examined to date appear to be Late Classic or possibly (in some cases) Early Postclassic. The number of types is quite limited, and there is a surprising lack of decorative elaboration; thus far there are no examples of the usual Late Classic polychrome types usually encountered at Maya lowland sites. The most striking omission, considering the purported close ties to nearby Copan, is the lack of Copador pottery, the diagnostic Late Classic ware of Copan (Longyear 1952).

The pottery picture at Quirigua contrasts with that emerging from the surrounding valley. The Site-Periphery Program and the Valley Survey of Timothy Nowak have both revealed considerable ceramic diversity. A range of Preclassic, Early Classic and Postclassic wares, all absent or feebly represented in the site-core, are present in the valley.

Further testing at Quirigua and the surrounding area should establish whether or not this apparent disparity in ceramic distribution is real. If the pattern is substantiated, the pottery evidence should provide information concerning Quirigua's temporal position (was Quirigua solely a Late Classic entity, what were its immediate origins, and was there Postclassic occupation at the site?), its degree of socio-political integration with the rest of the lower Motagua valley, and its relationship to Copan.

SITE CONSOLIDATION AND RENOVATION

Some 65 years in existence, the "Quirigua Park" of approximately 34 fenced hectares appears to have long presented a problem in maintenance. In 1933 O.G. Ricketson offered a proposal (unpublished) as to how this might be efficiently achieved, but this plan was never implemented. In 1971, however, the opening of a road to the site seems to have coincided with a conscientious effort by INGUAT to rectify the effects of what one surmises were years of increasing neglect. The old, large metal signs next to each monument and the

protective fences around them were refurbished; monuments obscured by mosses were cleaned; the site was bushed and the grass-covered Great Plaza cut; a *guardian* was installed, and various facilities for tourists were constructed. As mentioned earlier, the north central staircase of the Acropolis evidently was roughly reconstructed at this time. Cement benches were introduced in 1973 into the area of the Great Plaza. As a result of the donation in 1974 of the Park land to the government by the Del Monte Corporation, successor to the United Fruit Company in its ownership, responsibility for Quirigua legally devolved upon the Instituto de Antropología e Historia.

What amounts to a plan for the Park was designed collaboratively by Instituto personnel and the Project in 1975. Implementing this plan depends on funding a Park staff of sufficient size to guard and maintain it literally on a 24-hour basis, given the touristic traffic and general availability of the site. There is agreement that, with adequate guards (and Park rules publicly visible), the fences could be removed from about the monuments. To improve the aesthetics further, the signs for each monument could be removed and, as a guide to visitors, a simple descriptive leaflet be made available at the Park's entrance. Such a leaflet was prepared in 1975 jointly by the Project and Vivian Broman Morales and printed in Spanish and English by the Tikal Association.

Many monuments are imperiled by adjacent trees, largely the markedly rot-prone and unstately *jobo*. Visually, the magnitude of both the Great Plaza and monuments is nearly lost among these trees. This matter is under study, as are others centering on how to improve drainage and how best to improve and display monuments often inundated, for instance, Monuments 23 and 24.

By contract, the Project is specifically responsible for structural consolidation and discretionary reconstruction. A major effort towards this end will be underway in the Acropolis in 1976. Exactly what might be done with Structure 1A-3 at the north end of the Great Plaza as well as among structures (1A-4 through 10) along its east side is still under consideration. Excavations and clearing within the Acropolis this year did verify that the Project would not need to quarry material, a necessary and enormously expensive task at Tikal. But there is a major problem that we had not entirely foreseen, namely the dismantling and resetting of masonry. For instance, the exterior building walls of Structure 1B-5, when excavated this year, were found to be largely "sprung" and torsioned despite being made of huge, heavy blocks of marble. At fault is the large amount of dense mud used by the Maya as wall fill, and the gradual effects of its periodic saturation and drying on the retaining exterior masonry.

Among the many issues of preservation and improvement at Quirigua, perhaps none is so commonly raised as that of the lichens and mosses which affect every monument and, in some cases, envelop them. Happily, Dr. Mason Hale, of the Department of Botany, U.S. National Museum, has undertaken the study and treatment of these growths (see *Quirigua Paper, No. 3*). Directly promoting the infestation of the monuments is the combination of saturated settings and excessive shade. It is well understood that elimination of the growths will be gradual and delicate, best coordinated with a program of lithic solidification.

REFERENCES CITED

Carr, R. F., and J. E. Hazard
  1961   Map of the Ruins of Tikal, El Peten, Guatemala. Tikal Reports, No. 11. Philadelphia: University
         Museum.

Graham, I.
  1967   Archaeological Explorations in El Peten, Guatemala. Middle America Research Institute, Publication 33.
         New Orleans: Tulane University.

Hammond, N.
  1972   Obsidian Trade Routes in the Mayan Area. Science 178: 1092-1093.

Hewett, E. L.
  1911   Two Seasons' Work in Guatemala. Bulletin of the Archaeological Institute of America 2: 117-134.

  1912   The Excavations at Quirigua in 1912. Bulletin of the Archaeological Institute of America 3: 163-171.

Longyear, J. M.
  1952   Copan Ceramics:A Study of Southeastern Maya Pottery. Carnegie Institution of Washington,
          Publication 597, Washington D.C.

Morley, S. G.
  1935   Guide Book to the Ruins of Quirigua. Carnegie Institution of Washington, Supplementary
          Publication 16, Washington, D. C.
  1937-38   The Inscriptions of Peten. Carnegie Institution of Washington, Publication 437, Washington, D.C.

Stromsvik, G.
  1952   The Ball Courts at Copan; with Notes on Courts at La Union, Quirigua, San Pedro Pinula and Asuncion
          Mita. Carnegie Institution of Washington, Publication 596, Contribution 55, Washington, D. C.

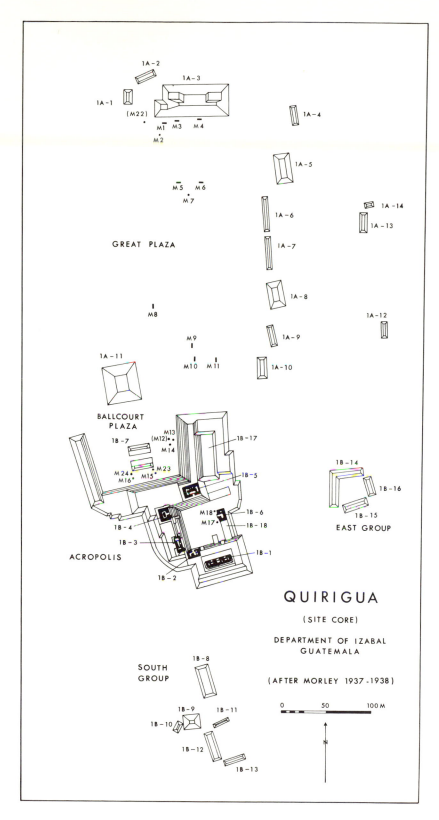

Figure 1. Map of Quirigua site-core modified from that published by Morley (1937-38: V, Pl. 214). Final Quirigua Project site-core map is furnished in the back pocket of this volume.

Figure 2. Excavations in Str. 1A-3 (Operation 2).
    a.   Clearing south face for axial trench. Monument 3 is at left.
    b.   Basal remains of south wall, Str. 1A-3-2nd.
    c.   Rear (north) wall, Str. 1A-3-2nd.
    d.   View east along the base of south wall, Str. 1A-3-2nd.

a

b   c

Figure 3. Excavations in Operation 4.
  a. Excavations around Monuments 15, 23 (right), 16 and 24 (left) as seen from the Acropolis.
  b. Monuments 24 (foreground) and 16 and supporting terrace.
  c. Terrace south of Monument 16, with flagstone (laja) terrace and earlier surfaces overlying alluvial soil.

27

a

b   c

Figure 4. Structure 1B-1 (Acropolis)
    a. View from north before clearing.
    b. After initial clearing, with bulldozer ridding Acropolis Plaza of accumulated debris from past excavations.
    c. Axial trench (Ops. 6G and 6I) in front of Str. 1B-1, seen from north.

a

b

c

Figure 5. Structure 1B-5 (Acropolis).
    a.   Clearing Str. 1B-5, as seen from Str. 1B-3.
    b.   Axial trench (Op. 6A) cut through debris overlying staircase, south side of Str. 1B-5.
    c.   View from southwest, after clearing of staircase, with north end of *Kinich Ahau* wall in foreground. Note debris remaining next to west wall of Str. 1B-5.

a

b

c

d

Figure 6. Excavation of *Kinich Ahau* wall (Acropolis)

    a.   Looking west at trench (Op. 6F) between Strs. 1B-3 and 1B-4, where wall was later discovered.

    b.   View south along wall during excavation. Note that south end of wall is better preserved than north end.

    c.   Southernmost *Kinich Ahau* mask, with Strs. 1B-5 and 1B-6 visible in background.

    d.   Close-up of mask of *Kinich Ahau*.

a

b

Figure 7. Quirigua Group A.
   a. Aerial view from east.
   b. Aerial view from southwest. Note old excavation in principal structure.

a

b

Figure 8. Quirigua Groups B and C.
  a. Aerial view of Group B, from northeast, with Monument 19 visible at center. Note traces of several recent drainage ditches.
  b. Aerial view of Group C, from east. Monument 25 (not visible) is midway between the two conspicuous mounds. Quirigua River and Atlantic Highway (CA9) in distance.

CONTROL OF THE LICHENS
ON THE MONUMENTS OF QUIRIGUA

by
Mason E. Hale, Jr.

INTRODUCTION

The civilization of the Classic lowland Maya is famous for its accomplishments in a variety of spheres, from calendric calculation and hieroglyphic writing, to complex masonry architecture, to ceramic decoration and relief carving in stone. In the case of stone carving, nowhere are the accolades more justified than in the southeastern elite centers of Copan and—despite the disparaging remarks of Scherzer (1936)—Quirigua (Morley 1920, 1937-38; Robicsek 1972). Unfortunately, however, these magnificent monuments have suffered much disfigurement over the centuries. Beginning with the ancient Maya themselves, countless people have—for a variety of reasons—defaced or broken the sculptures. Falling trees have toppled and smashed them. But, at Quirigua, some of the most pervasive and stealthy destruction has been wrought by much tinier agents in the form of lichens, mosses, and algae.

Whereas most of the Maya monuments are sculpted from limestone, the majority at Quirigua are sandstone (the remainder are rhyolite or schist). The latter stones—especially in the hot, humid and shady environment of Quirigua Park—are particularly susceptible to colonization by lichens and other botanical growths. These microscopic plant forms attach themselves to the surface of the stone and, as they spread, progressively weaken the surface. The result is that, if allowed to grow unchecked, these organisms will effectively "erase" the sculpture.

Fortunately the carving at Quirigua was done in relatively deep relief. And now, as part of the University Museum's current archaeological program at that site, work has begun to reclaim the Quirigua monuments from their biological encrustations. Since past efforts at such reclamation have been confined largely to gravestones and other carved stone in Europe, the present project represents pioneer research both in the New World and in tropical environments.

APPROACHES TO TREATMENT

There are basically two ways to remove the lichens—mechanically and chemically. Mechanical removal, by brushing or scraping, is painstaking but gives immediate results. With care this technique can be put to profitable use, as demonstrated in 1975 for preliminary recording of Monuments 23 and 24. But residual propagules inevitably remain and will, untreated, eventually form an even denser cover than the one originally removed. The advantage of chemical removal is that the growths are actually killed: all propagules are destroyed, and the dead plants either fall away, probably within a year, or can be brushed off with a soft hand brush without further damage to the rock surface.

Even the latter method of cleaning the monuments will not, however, eliminate lichens forever. Microscopic propagules are carried by wind and rain over long distances and will land on stone surfaces, start growing, and eventually recover the monuments. Judging from data on colonization of trees by lichens in temperate regions, it is estimated that primary invasion of newly cleaned surfaces at Quirigua would take about three years and visible growth would occur in three to five years. Photographs of various plots in 1973 provide a base for estimating the growth rates of lichens actually growing on the Quirigua monuments. For example, *Dirinaria picta*, a closely attached, rather persistent foliose species, is growing at the rate of 3.2 mm/year in radius. *Chiodecton antillarum*, the conspicuous crust on Monument 11, grows even more rapidly, about 4.5 mm/year. To put these rates in perspective, a colony of *Chiodecton* 10 mm in diameter would attain a diameter of nearly 100 mm in just ten years.

The indicated procedure, then, is clearly a combination of chemical removal of growths—to produce a biologically sterile surface—and treatment with sealers and stone stabilizers to retard recolonization and solidify surfaces. The main objection to this method is that it is much slower than simple mechanical removal, and there are no immediate results; it is estimated that a full year would be needed just to clean a monument completely. But it should be obvious as well that, ultimately, combined chemical removal and stabilization is the only effective approach.

EXPERIMENTS AT QUIRIGUA

The monument preservation program at Quirigua began in April 1973 with a preliminary assessment of the species of growths present and the extent of their colonization. The growths are primarily lichens, with lesser amounts of mosses and blue-green algae. Among the lichens, a number of species is represented, including *Chiodecton antillarum*, *Leptotrema santense*, *Dirinaria picta*, and *Parmotrema* sp. The main alga found was *Oscillatoria*.

In February 1975, through funds provided by Mr. S. Dillon Ripley, Secretary of the Smithsonian Institution, the author and Dr. Theodore Esslinger, also of the U.S. National Museum, Smithsonian Institution, were able to return to begin experimental treatment of Monuments 2 and 11. Selection of these particular monuments was intended to provide contrast in location as well as in encrustation. Monument 2, one of the so-called "zoomorphs," is exposed to considerable sunshine during the day. Monument 11, on the other hand, had the greatest coverage of lichens among the stelae—in part, at least, because it is situated at and heavily shaded by the forest border.

To begin treatment, portions of the two monuments were marked off in four 1-meter quadrats. Then the quadrats were assigned to spraying conditions according to a 2 x 2 experimental design. That is, two biocidal solutions were tested, each being applied either once or twice to both monuments. The two solutions used (Richardson 1973) were household bleach (chlorox) diluted 1:4 with water, and a 5% aqueous solution of polyborate (borax). With both of these the biocidal effect is probably achieved by killing off algal cells in the lichen and green leaf cells of mosses. Borax has poorer wetting qualities and had to be applied at the rate of 500 cc/m^2 to achieve good wetting; chlorox was easier to apply and only 300 cc/m^2 were needed. It appears that some lichens such as *Leptotrema santense* are sufficiently water repellent to resist the effects of a single treatment. A detergent should be added in future treatments.

After the close of the 1975 season, under initial funds from a 3-year grant from the National Geographic Society, the author returned in July 1975 to brush off dead growths and inspect the overall results of treatment. Color photographs were taken on this visit—as on previous ones—to document changes in plant cover. All prints and transparencies are kept on file in the laboratory of the Department of Botany, U.S. National Museum, Smithsonian Institution.

RESULTS

Monument 2 is exposed to considerable sunshine during the day. The top is covered by a dense black coating of a blue-green alga, *Oscillatoria*. The sides are covered with various crustose lichens, foliose but tightly adnate *Dirinaria picta*, and small colonies of *Parmotrema* and mosses.

Two one meter plots were laid out on the top of Monument 2, one facing west and one east. Borax was sprayed on the east slope. The alga turned greenish and dried out within 30 minutes. The west side was sprayed with chlorox. On the return visit in July it was almost impossible to detect any effect. A careful comparison of photographs showed, however, that some thinning of the *Oscillatoria* had occurred. This algal cover is obviously very resistant and stronger solutions will be needed for spraying.

The west side of Monument 2 had considerable coverage by foliose lichens, mosses, and crusts. It was sprayed once with borax. After 4 months there was little evidence of lichen loss, and vigorous brushing merely removed the larger lichens and mosses. In this case a second treatment will be needed.

The predominant lichen on the vertical front of the monument is *Dirinaria picta*. The surface was sprayed twice with chlorox in February and dried out quickly. By July many colonies had started to crumble at the edges or thin out at the center.

The *Chiodecton antillarum* and the mosses on Monument 11 were very sensitive to the sprays and could be brushed off easily four months later. *Leptotrema santense* appeared to be alive and could not be removed with a soft brush. The extensive white endolithic crust did not seem to be affected, but more time will be needed to assess possible damage since even when dead this white crust will tend to persist for some time.

The north side of Monument 11 had scattered *Chiodecton* and *Leptotrema*, several small moss-covered areas, and a general background of the sterile white endolithic crust. It receives considerable sun in the afternoon and appears to be very dry and crusty compared with the shaded sides. It was sprayed once with chlorox. Brushing by hand later removed the larger lichens and mosses but seemed to have no effect on the endolithic crusts.

The east side of the monument is shaded by the adjacent forest and for this reason retains moisture long after a rain storm. It was covered with *Chiodecton* and *Leptotrema* and a few mosses. Treatment consisted of two sprayings at a four-hour interval with borax. The *Chiodecton* turned red immediately, a result of the oxidation of the lichenic acid contained in the plant body. The vertical half of the quadrat toward the north was washed with water until no red diffused out; this treatment had no effect on later results. In July 1975 the *Chiodecton* and mosses were easily removed with a hand brush. The *Leptotrema* persisted as white patches.

The south side resembled the east side in heavy coverage of *Chiodecton* and *Leptotrema*. It also tends to be heavily shaded and to retain moisture. Chlorox was applied twice but was not washed out with water later. The reaction is essentially similar to that on the east side. The *Chiodecton* brushed off easily, leaving only scattered colonies of the more persistent *Leptotrema*.

The west side approximated the north side very closely in dry, crusty appearance and more scattered coverage with crustose lichens. It was sprayed once with borax. Later brushing cleaned much of the surface although the endolithic white crusts persisted. Many details of sculpture on this side emerged.

On the whole, the experiments have been successful and have shown the efficacy of a preliminary treatment combining spraying with later brush removal of dead plant matter. Differential resistance of the various species seems, at this point, related as much to degree of exposure to sunlight as to variation in treatment.

FUTURE WORK

In 1976—thanks again to the support of the National Geographic Society—the program of monument cleaning will continue with extensified spraying, increasing both the number of monuments treated and the variety of solutions used. For example, several British-made solutions promise growth-retarding residues in addition to immediately biocidal agents. And, hopefully, a more successful algicide will be found. We also plan to compare more rigorously the effects of simple mechanical cleaning (brushing) on both living and freshly sprayed growths.

Not until 1977 will we be in a position to devote serious attention to the application of stabilizers and sealants. But by that time we should have learned a great deal about how to control the growths. And in so doing we see hope of halting at least this aspect of the relentless destruction of the monuments at Quirigua.

REFERENCES CITED

Morley, S.G.
  1920   The Inscriptions at Copan. Carnegie Institution of Washington, Publication 219, Washington, D.C.
  1937-38   The Inscriptions of Peten. Carnegie Institution of Washington, Publication 437, Washington, D.C.
Richardson, B.A.
  1973   Control of Biological Growths. Stone Industries 8 (2): 2-6.
Robicsek, F.
  1972   Copan, Home of the Mayan Gods. New York: Museum of the American Indian, Heye Foundation.
Scherzer, C.
  1936   A Visit to Quirigua. Maya Research 3 (1): 92-101.

Figure 1. West side of Monument 11 before treatment. Photography by Mason E. Hale Jr.

Figure 2. West side of Monument 11 after spraying with borax solution and brush removal of dead plant material. Photography by Mason E. Hale, Jr.

QUIRIGUA ALTAR L
(MONUMENT 12) [1]

by
Linton Satterthwaite

Altars L, Q and R (Monuments 12, 17; and 18) at Quirigua differ greatly from other monuments at the site and have been assigned chronological positions near the beginning of the sequence by Morley. Only in the case of Altar L is the inscription legible, and that does not record an Initial Series (IS) or a normally stated Period End (PE) date. I think, nevertheless, we can make a good case for 9.12.0.0.0 as its dedicatory date, rather than Morley's 9.14.13.12.0 with three question marks. His discussion of the three monuments, with references to illustrations, will be found in his *Inscriptions of Peten, Vol. II* (1937-38: 94-98; 102-105). Maudslay's drawing of Altar L is reproduced as Figure 1 (Maudslay 1889-1902).

These are the only round altars at the site, agreeing closely in size, which is small, and in presenting a centered human figure, seated cross-legged, with glyphs at one or both sides of the figure. All were found in the Main Group, though Altar L seems to have been moved from its original position when first seen by Catherwood. No stelae are known with which they might have been once associated, and the presumption is that they spoke for themselves. In each case there were glyph blocks which could have declared the dedicatory period-ends in normal PE style, and only in the case of Altar L is it certain that this was not done.

Within this group of basically similar altars, the differences in age are presumably not very great. While minor differences may be linked to passage of time, alternative postulates seem admissible.

Altars Q and R, much eroded, clearly form a pair. This might or might not mean that they were dedicated at precisely the same time. On each, the figure sits on an oval frame, likened to a "cushion" by Morley. The photographs suggest that on Altar R there were three glyphs within this frame. If so, this was presumably the case with Altar Q; but the frame visually separated these supposed glyphs from those beside the figures. In contrast, on Altar L the figure sits directly on two glyphs. It seems possible to believe that the oval frame is omitted here because the figure sits on the fourth and fifth blocks of a continuous inscription. On this theory, its ten blocks were arranged in an irregular "U" form because of exigencies of space.

The figures and the glyphs of Altars Q and R appear in a four-lobed field defined by a scalloped frame. On Altar L the field is circular, being, in fact, the interior area of a giant day-sign cartouche, complete with trinal support and associated day-number 10. These strikingly different peripheral treatments do not necessarily reflect changing fashion, though of course they may do so. The frame and the giant day-sign are firmly linked at Caracol, British Honduras, where they appear on the same stone as early as 9.8.0.0.0 (Satterthwaite 1951).

Proskouriakoff considers Altar L to be a variant of

---

[1]This paper was written in the mid-1960's, as a development from Dr. Satterthwaite's analyses of the monuments of Caracol, Belize (formerly British Honduras). Although not a direct result of Quirigua Project research, the essay is clearly relevant to our work, and Dr. Satterthwaite has graciously allowed us to include it in our publication series. Since the paper was written, further work has been done (e.g., Graham 1972) which bears on some of the issues raised herein; also the monument-designation system at Quirigua has been modified (see *Quirigua Paper, No. 2*, this volume). Rather than impose our own editorial revisions, however, we have preferred to present the paper as originally written.

Late Classic, the other two being assigned more specifically to the "Dynamic" phase of Late Classic (Proskouriakoff 1950: 194). Her conclusions are presumably based on the human figures. Her Late Classic Period begins at 9.8.0.0.0, and its Dynamic Phase at 9.16.0.0.0, but these dates are, of course, generalizations not claimed to set precise limits at each and every site. She does not use Morley's doubtful precise date for Altar L, nor his datings of the other two as "between 9.16.0.0.0 and 9.19.0.0.0." So far as one can tell, she might agree with him that Altar L is the earliest of the three. It seems to me highly improbable that any of these three modest altars was carved during the period beginning at 9.16.0.0.0 with a tremendous burst of sculptural activity in the Main Group.

Morley's readings of Altar L, and suggested new ones, are summarized below for comparison and then discussed.

GLYPHS	MORLEY READINGS	SUGGESTED READINGS
Inner Glyphs A1-A2	(9.13.13.6.11 ???) 9 Chuen 14 Tzec	(9.11.0.11.11 ?) 9 Chuen 14 Tzec
A3-D1		Its (the katun's) day 10 Ahau ??
Giant Glyph	10 (?) (not explained)	(9.12.0.0.0 ?) (Katun) 10 (Ahau)
Outer Glyphs G5-G4	(9.14.13.12.0 ???) 12 Ahau 3 Xul	(9.12.0.17.0 ?) 12 Ahau 3 Xul

DISCUSSION

In the new reading the giant glyph is given the same meaning as it seems to have at Caracol. There the giant glyph was (probably always) definitely shown as *Ahau*. Here, where this is not done, surely it is *Ahau* which was understood. The best explanation of these giant statements at Caracol is that they name a katun. This could be the katun marked by the monument but probably might also be the katun current as of some stated division of the katun (Satterthwaite 1951,1965).

If we are correct in our reading of a katun name, since there is no evidence of an associated stela and no ordinary PE date on the altar, 9.12.0.0.0 was presumably the dedicatory date. On the principle that non-dedicatory dates usually precede, but may slightly "over-run" the dedicatory one, I have shifted Morley's Long Count positions for the two Calendar Round (CR) dates back by one CR period.

I turn to the inner inscription. The prefix in A3 looks like a normal bracket with two dots in Morley's photo, the best one. Although Maudslay draws it differently, I follow Morley in considering it one of the orthodox "ending signs." Thompson (1950) has shown that this bracket prefix cannot mean "end," but represents the sound "u," and that it might express the possessive, as in our reading. It might also change a cardinal to an ordinal number. We could amend Morley's "End of Kin 11" to "11th Kin." But why should valuable space be used to record the obvious fact that *Chuen* follows 11 days after *Ahau*? Further, the drawing, this time fairly well confirmed by photographs, does not show two bars and one dot at the right of A3, but the bars and a peculiar bifurcated element. Loss of incised details might cause mis-drawing of the "*u*-bracket." Scratches on a dot would probably be recognized as such. The best reading seems to be 10, with this bifurcated element still to be explained. It might mean that the number, in an unexpected position to the right of the *kin* glyph, is nevertheless to be read with it; but it might just as well mean that, despite its juxtaposition to the *kin* sign, it is to be read with the next glyph, D1, as is assumed in our reading.

This next glyph looks much like a rare form of the day-sign *Ahau*, without cartouche, used on Stela 12 at Uaxactun, and considered to be an archaism there by Morley (Morley 1937-38: I, 155, 225). Here it lacks the normal trinal support or "pedestal" but has affixes which conceivably may be an earlier and elaborated version of Thompson's "Postfix A," which is the "owl plume" affix of Beyer (1937). Along with *ben-ich* prefix and *Ahau*, this affix is common at Chichen Itza. The combination, with a day-number, gives the name of the current katun. The "owl plume" may, however, appear in such a context without the prefix (Beyer 1937: Figs. 680, 681, 694). See Thompson (1950: 192,198, 203, 282) for examples and discussions of what I call "katun-naming" expressions in early and late inscriptions. His findings are a principle prop for the interpretation of the giant *Ahau* glyphs at Caracol. Our reading of the two bars with this glyph makes sense, if it really is a day-sign with affix, whether that affix is "owl plume" or not.

As Beyer and Thompson show, at Chichen Itza the *kin* sign may be used as a determinant, giving notice that a *tzolkin* date is being given. Examples indexed by Thompson show that it may appear before or after the *tzolkin*-date part of a CR date, but apparently not after the month portion, when the CR date is being elaborated. Presumably it might also be used as "day indicator" before a *tzolkin* date as katun-namer, and thus happen to come after a month sign, and it is so interpreted in our reading. Beyer shows at least one "day indicator" with the "katun-namer," the *kin* sign coming after (Beyer 1937:Fig. 648). Neither Morley's interpretation nor ours accounts for three dots which seem to appear *below* the *kin* sign.

This reading of A3-D1 is given two question marks, but it makes an understandable clause of the first four glyphs of a supposedly continuous inner inscription. The unexpected position of the two bars becomes explainable as due to the small U-shaped space into which the glyphs have to be crowded; and an unusual minor element takes on meaning. It agrees with the interpretation of the giant glyph, and so tends to confirm it.

If our dating of Altar L is correct, the "dynamic" qualities noted in Altars Q and R by Proskouriakoff probably mean that they are later, as Morley thought; but they might still precede the remarkable sculptural development from 9.16.0.0.0 on at the Main Group. Using the katun yardstick, 9.13.0.0.0, 9.14.0.0.0 and 9.15.0.0.0 would be possibilities for Altars Q and R. If we think of all three small round altars as characterizing an earliest local period, one would look to the Peten-British Honduras area, rather than toward Copan, for the cultural ancestors of the original "founders."

REFERENCES CITED

Beyer, H.
1937   Studies on the Inscriptions of Chichen Itza. Carnegie Institution of Washington, Publication 483, Washington, D.C.

Graham, John A.
1972   The Hieroglyphic Inscriptions and Monumental Art of Altar de Sacrificios. Papers of the Peabody Museum, Vol. 64, No. 2. Cambridge: Harvard University.

Maudslay, A.P.
1889-1902 Archaeology. Biologia Centrali-Americana. 5 vols. London: Porter.

Morley, S.G.
1937-38   The Inscriptions of Peten. 5 vols. Carnegie Institution of Washington, Publication 437, Washington, D.C.

Proskouriakoff, T.
1950   A Study of Classic Maya Sculpture. Carnegie Institution of Washington, Publication 593, Washington, D.C.

Satterthwaite, L.
1951   Reconnaissance in British Honduras. Bulletin of the University Museum, Vol. 16, No. 1.
1965   Dates on the Monuments of Caracol, British Honduras. Manuscript, American Section, University Museum, University of Pennsylvania.

Thompson, J.E.S.
1950   Maya Hieroglyphic Writing: An Introduction. Carnegie Institution of Washington, Publication 589, Washington, D.C.

Figure 1. Monument 12 (Altar L), Quirigua.
Drawing by Annie Hunter, originally published by Maudslay (1889-1902: II, Fig. 49b). Reproduced by permission of Milpatron Publishing Corp., New York.

Figure 2. Monument 12 (Altar L), Quirigua.
   Photograph by Jesse L. Nusbaum (ca. 1910), previously published by Morley (1937-38: V, Pl. 173d). Reproduced
   by permission of the Museum of New Mexico, Santa Fe. Now located in Guatemala City, this monument is made
   of "whitish-gray stone" (probably rhyolite); Morley (1937-38: IV, 95) describes it as being 1.02 m in diameter with
   a thickness of about 25 cm.

THE QUIRIGUA PROJECT

1976 SEASON

by

Robert J. Sharer, Christopher Jones, Wendy Ashmore
and Edward M. Schortman

INTRODUCTION

The 1976 season of archaeological research at Quirigua lasted nearly four months, from mid-January to early May. Actual excavation commenced February 2 and continued until April 24 (12 weeks). The following report summarizes the results of this work. The January period was spent making preparatory arrangements. Two formal meetings were held in Guatemala City with the Instituto de Antropologia e Historia (IDAEH) during this time in order to present plans for the 1976 research program and to hear recommendations from the Instituto. During the same interval both the Project camp (Los Amates) and the Project compound (Quirigua) were opened, inventoried and renovated. After the closing of excavations in late April, a final meeting with the Instituto was held to report on the work completed and to turn over to the Instituto responsibility for the collections and facilities at Quirigua during the off-season period.

The 1976 field staff was composed of Robert Sharer (Field Director), Christopher Jones (Director of Site-Core Excavations), Mary Bullard (Laboratory Director), David Sedat (Administrative Director), Wendy Ashmore (Supervisor of Site-Periphery Program), Enrique Monterroso (Crew Foreman and Supervisor of Restoration), along with Daniel Milla-Villeda, Edward Schortman, and John Weeks (Student Field Assistants) and John Glavis (Volunteer Photographer). Marcelino Gonzalez served as Assessor on the part of IDAEH. Dr. Mason Hale (Smithsonian Institution) continued his advisory capacity in regard to the control of microflora (for the Monument Preservation and Recording Program), and Bruce Bevan (Museum Applied Science Center for Archaeology) conducted the magnetometer survey.

A maximum of 60 local laborers was employed for excavation and other tasks connected with the research program. In addition, up to 20 workmen were engaged in restoration.

As in 1975, financial support for research was furnished by both the University Museum (Francis Boyer Museum Fund) and the National Geographic Society. This year these agencies were joined by the National Science Foundation, which contributed about one-third of the research funds (BNS7602183). In addition, the Quirigua Project has been aided by contributions from several private benefactors, including Mr. Landon T. Clay and Mr. Alfred G. Zantzinger. As specified in the Project contract, the Government of Guatemala provided all funds connected with renovation and restoration of the site.

Two days after the 1976 excavations began, Guatemala suffered a devastating earthquake. The Project camp and the ruins of Quirigua are located immediately adjacent to the strike-slip fault running the length of the Motagua Valley which ruptured at 3:02 a.m. on February 4. While the epicenter of the quake, which was estimated at 7.5 on the Richter scale, has been tentatively located in the vicinity of Quirigua, the worst destruction of life and property occurred in the highland areas of the middle and upper Motagua drainage basins, southwest of the site. The basic reasons for this appear to be architectural: the majority of the buildings in the lower Motagua valley, including the Los Amates-Quirigua area, are constructed of wood with either thatch or metal roofs. Adobe structures, when found, are almost never roofed with tile. In contrast, the prevalent construction in the devastated middle and upper Motagua regions is adobe with heavy tile roofs.

Fortunately, there were no injuries to members of the Project. However, the quake and continuing after-shocks caused some structural damage to the Project camp (constructed of reinforced concrete block) and the Project compound at the ruins (a water tower was severely damaged). The ruins of Quirigua suffered more seriously; a full report of this damage will be issued in a future number of the *Quirigua Reports*.

As a consequence of the earthquake the Project's lines of communication and supply with Guatemala City were severed. Thanks to the efforts of Vivian Broman de Morales in Guatemala City and Elizabeth Sedat in Tactic, Alta Verapaz, shortwave calls were made to the

U.S. to inform families of staff members that all personnel were unhurt. Local telegraph service returned about two weeks after the quake, but the main road to Guatemala City was not reopened until April 22. Two staff members with families living in devastated areas (Monterroso and Sedat) were given emergency leave to journey to their homes. Fortunately, both learned that their families were safe, although Sedat's house in the Baja Verapaz was badly damaged. However, because of the dedication of all personnel, staff, and workers, the Project was able to improvise and to continue its research program throughout the emergency period.

The other major problem faced by the Project in 1976, inflation, continued to drain the funds in excess of all preliminary estimates. Costs of supplies and equipment, increased further by shortages in the wake of the earthquake, soared beyond 1975 levels. Despite these difficulties, the 1976 season was judged by all involved to have been highly successful, and a great deal of significant archaeological data was obtained.

OBJECTIVES FOR THE 1976 RESEARCH SEASON

The principal objectives of the 1976 season were pursued through five integrated research programs. The first of these, the mapping program, had as its goal the completion of the 1:2000 site map begun in 1975. The core excavation program, concerned with excavations within the Quirigua Park, was aimed at continuing the 1975 work in the Acropolis and in Str.1A-3, along with initiating excavations in several untested structures, in order to understand the basic construction sequence of these entities. The goals of the site-periphery program were to complete the identification and mapping of sites outside the site-core (within an area of 95 km²). The pottery analysis program was begun in 1976 to formulate a basic typology to assess excavated or surface-collected lots, leading toward a

preliminary temporal and functional evaluation of occupation in and around Quirigua. The monument preservation and recording program continued its objectives of controlling the growth of microflora and of recording (via photography, molds and rubbings) the complete corpus of monuments and inscriptions at Quirigua. In addition, a magnetometer survey was undertaken to assist the settlement, core-excavation and monument-preservation programs in locating buried structures or monuments.

In connection with the research programs, the Quirigua restoration program made substantial progress in 1976, operating with Guatemalan government funds under a renegotiated agreement with the Instituto de Antropologia e Historia.

RESULTS OF RESEARCH 1976

SITE-MAPPING PROGRAM

The Quirigua site map was begun in 1975 (see *Quirigua Paper, No. 2,* this volume) and completed during the 1976 season (enclosed inside back cover). The 1976 work carried out by Weeks and Schortman involved obtaining contour information at 0.5-m

intervals for the area within the Quirigua Park, using plane table and alidade. In addition, outlying structures within one grid square of the park were plotted on the 1:2000 map. These have received the standard structure designations based upon the map grid system.

The completed map is included in the present volume.

SITE-CORE PROGRAM

The 1976 excavations in the site-core (the large-scale architecture within Quirigua Park) comprised both continuations of 1975 work and a set of new excavations. Continuing work included investigation of the great northern mound, Str. 1A-3, as well as deep probing in the Acropolis, especially on its western and southern sides, to determine stratigraphic relationships of its various structural features. New excavations were begun in the Ballcourt Plaza, in the east side of the Acropolis Plaza, and in three structures bordering the Great Plaza (Strs. 1A-8, 10 and 11). All of the excavations will continue in 1977 and thus the following account is a progress report, emphasizing the complexities of the problems and only tentatively stating possible solutions.

THE ACROPOLIS

The Acropolis represents the largest and most complex construction at Quirigua. Work completed to date indicates that during its various stages of growth, the Acropolis was expanded both laterally and vertically, the latter through superimposed construction. Although we presently understand only a portion of this building activity, we already face a practical problem with respect to designating the various construction stages in reports such as this. The Quirigua Project is following the general construction designation system developed at Tikal (see *Quirigua Paper, No. 1,* this volume). But until we achieve a fuller understanding of the building activity in the Acropolis, most construction components will continue to be designated by the field system using "nonsense" names (such as BOM, CHAC, RAT, ZIP, and so forth). These labels are attached to each discrete building component, for example, walls, floors, fill, etc. Eventually, each component will receive a formal (Unit) designation. But instead of introducing a confusing array of temporary field labels into this report, the following discussions will utilize descriptive terms, such as "western stairway," "early eastern platform," and so forth, except for those few structures already formally designated. A fundamental problem that we already anticipate involves our ultimate understanding of the Acropolis as a total entity. Is the Acropolis to be seen as a single, complex, developing platform, composed of a single series of units, supporting a series of structures throughout its growth? Or do we view it as a group of discrete platforms, each composed of a separate series of constructional units, supporting structures that, due to growth through time, became more or less merged into a single entity? We anticipate that future excavation will resolve this basic issue.

Work in the Acropolis during 1976 covered the entire field season. The investigations were under the direction of Jones, assisted by Weeks and Milla-Villeda. The report begins by describing the excavations on the north side of the Acropolis, in the area of the Ballcourt Plaza, and then considers the work in the Acropolis proper (see Fig. 2).

The Ballcourt Plaza

The 1976 excavations in the area of the Acropolis began in the "Ballcourt Plaza," or what Morley called the "Ceremonial Plaza," the flat area bounded on the north by Str. 1A-11, and on the west, south and east by three staircases leading to the Acropolis platforms (Morley's Terraces XII, XIII, and XIV; see Fig. 2 or Morley 1935: Fig. 3). The decision to begin the season in this plaza was dictated by its important location as the transition area between the Acropolis, with its complex stratigraphy, and the dated monuments north of the Acropolis. Furthermore, it was thought that restoration work could begin here and move to the Acropolis in later seasons.

Excavation concentrated on the massive staircases on the east side of the Ballcourt Plaza (Fig. 2:h) and on the southeast terraced corner of the plaza. Because of the tremors following the February 4 earthquake, excavations remained shallow, but a basic stratigraphy emerged. It was discovered that the east stairs of the plaza preceded Str. 1B-5-1st (Fig. 2:n), the large building facing south into the Acropolis Plaza. An east-west trench in the center of this stairway revealed two phases of large-stone block construction. The earlier construction had been ripped out, except for the lowermost course along the entire width of the present stairway, and some stones of terrace facings at the north end of the stairway, as well as terraces with sloping walls and apron mouldings at the south end of the stairs. These latter terraces continue south under the terraces of the Str. 1B-5 pyramid. Since they reach the basal level of Str. 1B-5-2nd (Fig. 2:m), found in 1975 under Str. 1B-5-1st, they are probably associated with it, though not necessarily built at the same time.

The building of the second and latest east stairway apparently occurred at the time of the construction of Str. 1B-5-1st, for not only do the lower terraces of Str. 1B-5-1st's "pyramid" abut the apron terraces of the earlier stairway, covering their southern portions, but also the masonry on the high uppermost terrace of the pyramid dovetails with the latest uppermost terrace and the new stairway. Furthermore, no break or change can be seen in the latest stairway from top to bottom. Thus it appears that the stairway and its platform were raised one terrace level in height to correspond with the new elevation of Str. 1B-5-1st, built over Str. 1B-5-2nd.

A frontal terrace (Fig. 2:g) for the new east stairway was a part of this second phase. Its terrace wall, usually about 1 m high, was traced by selective excavation along the western and northern sides of the stairway platform. On its axis was discovered a large sandstone slab (Fig. 2:d) which may have served as a pedestal for one of the three monuments found in that vicinity in the 19th century (see below). To the south, the later "zoomorph terrace" (Fig. 2:f) supporting Monuments 15 and 16 (Fig. 2:c,b) abuts this terrace.

The east stairway leads to a platform that sustains a long low structure platform (Str. 1B-17; Fig 2:j) which probably once supported a perishable building. Its western stairway has five steps running most of the length of the front and is flanked by side terraces, repeating the flanking terraces of the platform stairway below it. The structure was not penetrated, nor was the back of the structure and platform excavated. No cut stone blocks were seen in back, and the surface is covered by cobbles suggesting the same unfinished, or robbed, state seen on the rear of Str. 1A-3 at the north end of the Great Plaza (see *Quirigua Paper, No. 2*). Large indentations into the fill at the southeast corner of the platform suggest extensive robbing operations in that area.

The terraces sustaining Str. 1B-5-1st are abutted by a third large construction, the great south stairway (Fig. 2:i) which leads from the south side of the Ballcourt Plaza up to the large flat platform west of Str. 1B-5. During this ancient construction, some of the terraces were partially torn away, but others were incorporated into the stairway plan. One was even lengthened 2 m to meet the new stairway. At the same time, the lower two terraces were covered by three terraces, made of white marble and grey volcanic stones. The "zoomorph terrace," on which sit Monuments 15 and 16 (Zoomorphs O and P), clearly runs under this great stairway, suggesting strongly that these "zoomorphs" were in place when this final construction was undertaken, although detection of a stratigraphic link between the monuments and the terrace was foiled in 1975 by previous excavations around and under the monuments.

Thus, as a result of the 1976 excavations, three sequent phases of construction were clearly seen in the terraced corner of the Ballcourt Plaza and could be at least tentatively associated with hieroglyphic dates. The first phase, the early east stairway, precedes the axial pedestal stone which probably sustained one or more of the three monuments found at the base of the stair: Monument 13 (M), bearing dates probably corresponding to 9.15.0.0.0 and 9.15.3.2.0, both ca. A.D. 730; Monument 14 (N), bearing no date or inscription but similar to Monument 13 in being made of a white rhyolite stone which contrasts with the sandstone of the later monuments; and finally Monument 12 (L), now in Guatemala City in the National Museum, but originally found near the others. (Catherwood perhaps saw Monument 12 supported on the other two!) For Monument 12, Morley suggested a date of 9.14.13.12.0, but Satterthwaite has recently suggested 9.12.0.0.0 (see *Quirigua Paper, No. 4*). The critical pedestal stone was placed on the plaza floor abutting the first phase construction and is enveloped, but not completely buried, by the floor of the subsequent frontal terrace of the second phase. Thus it is earlier than or contemporary with the second phase, which consists of the new east stairway, the frontal terrace, and the terraces supporting Str. 1B-5.

Dated monuments are also associated with the third and last construction documented in the Ballcourt Plaza, the south stairway. Since this stairway clearly follows construction of the "zoomorph terrace" (and by implication follows placement of the monuments themselves), it can tentatively be assigned a post-9.18.5.0.0 date, the dates of Monuments 16 and 24 (Zoomorph P and its Altar). In sum, the sequence between the east and south stairways corresponds to the sequence of hieroglyphic dates between the eastern and southern groups of monuments. That is, the earlier phase of construction of the eastern staircase appears to be either earlier than or contemporary with the period of 9.12.0.0.0 to 9.15.3.2.0 (A.D. 672-731), while the southern staircase is probably later than 9.18.5.0.0 (A.D. 795). Thus, the stratigraphy places Str. 1B-5-1st (built during the second phase) somewhere in the period between 9.15.0.0.0 and construction of the south stairway, in the era of the giant stelae and of Quirigua's dominant ruler, Cauac Sky, and his successors.

No excavations were undertaken in the western part of the Ballcourt Plaza or in the ballcourt itself (Str. 1B-7; Fig. 2:a). However, the ballcourt is an important feature and should be excavated in 1977, as soon as the great amate tree now in its center has been felled.

After three weeks of excavation and recording, a plan for consolidation and partial reconstruction work in this area was prepared and presented to the Instituto de Antropologia e Historia. The Project recommended beginning work immediately on the terraces of the plaza's southeast corner. These terraces lend themselves well to the consolidation work, since many of the massive blocks remain in their original positions. Once these are stabilized and fallen blocks reset, the corner terraces will be striking to behold. The south stairway, partially re-set by the Instituto de Turismo de Guatemala several years ago, must be re-set yet again. The recommendation called for the eastern stairway to remain untouched except for continual maintenance. The stones have slumped more or less in place, making the original stair lines easy to imagine and impressing the viewer with the power of both the original massive block construction and its subsequent movements. The stair blocks are also very stable at present. Selected walls at the corners of the northern end of the staircase and on the front of Str. 1B-17 were also slated for restoration, but it was recommended that the rest of the platform be left as it is. Included in the plan was provision for the clearing of the Ballcourt Plaza of the up to 1 m of silt laid down by river inundations. The job will not be as massive as it might seem, because the eastern terrace lies so near the surface, and hopefully a front-end loader can be secured to speed up removal of this 30-cm silt layer as well as the deeper silts covering the rest of the area. It was agreed that the ballcourt be cleared of silt and restored after excavation, thus forming the western limits of the clearing operation. Drainage would be provided by clearing the terrace wall as it extends north and east, expanding the existing drainage ditch. In sum, the operation would not be extensive or expensive and would restore the sculptured monuments to their original impressive setting between the ballcourt and the south stairway, clear the terrace walls and surfaces, as well as provide adequate drainage for the monuments, presently flooded every rainy season.

In this plan, the stairways and terraces flanking the plaza are thought of as focusing the eye down onto the playing field of the low-sided ballcourt, thereby serving as viewing stands for the game. The architecture would therefore become functionally understandable to any viewer. Furthermore, it is hoped that the three phases of construction will be apparent as they meet and overlap in the southeast corner of the Plaza. Without a great deal of expense, the restoration in this important area of Quirigua between the Great Plaza and the Acropolis will help develop a visual feeling of considerable grandeur and variety.

This plan was accepted by the Instituto de Antropologia e Historia and is now being carried out under the able direction of Enrique Monterroso. By the time research ceased, the corner terraces were cleared of debris and work had begun on stabilizing and re-setting the blocks.

Structure 1B-5 (Fig. 2:n)

For the Acropolis proper, the 1976 excavations will be described counterclockwise from the north side of the Acropolis Plaza, to the western platforms, followed by those of the south and finally the east.

The largest building at Quirigua, Str. 1B-5, is located on the north side of the Acropolis and was extensively excavated in 1975. In 1976, the large roof stones of the rear chamber, badly collapsed by the Feb. 4 earthquake, were removed and recorded in preparation for restoration. Room step-ups and benches were checked for evidence of secondary construction. Interestingly enough, none was found. The discovery of northern and western faces of terraces sustaining the structure demonstrated that the building was once a more isolated entity than at present, before the mass of the platform covering Strs. 1B-Sub.2 and 3 (Fig. 2:k,l; see below) was placed against its western side. The uppermost terrace, about 2.80 m high, extends along both the north and west sides of the structure, but the four lower terraces are each only about 1.40 m high and do not continue south to the Acropolis Plaza. The high upper terrace is plain, but the lower ones have a projecting cornice on top. All are perfectly vertical, in contrast to earlier sloping terrace faces in the Acropolis.

In 1975, the eastern end of a buried structure was encountered in the axial trench under the front room of Str. 1B-5. The western end of this building, now called Str. 1B-5-2nd (Fig. 2:m), was uncovered in 1976 in a long north-south trench west of the substructure wall of Str. 1B-5-1st. The western end of the buried structure had been ripped out during construction of Str. 1B-5-1st, but the front and back walls and the entire western end of the interior room were discovered, allowing a confident reconstruction of the building plan. Str. 1B-5-2nd is a south-facing building measuring 7.6 m wide by about 16 m long, with a single room 3.5 by ca. 12 m. The building stands on a platform with a wide southern stairway and sloping corner terraces. In 1975, a deep-relief stucco human figure was found on the east end of the south facade just below the medial molding, but no new stucco work was found this year. The trenches exposing this structure were back-filled in preparation for the restoration work planned for Str. 1B-5-1st.

Structure 1B-Sub. 3 (Fig. 2:l)

West of Str. 1B-5, three corners of another buried structure (Str. 1B-Sub.3) were encountered under the present flat surface of the north Acropolis platform (Morley's Terrace XIII). The building was fortunately buried intact up to its original roof plaster (at least in its northeast corner) by the cobble fill of the later platform, thus providing us with the only complete Quirigua building profile thus far discovered. The building seems to face north instead of south and rests at a lower level than Str. 1B-5-2nd. However, it is almost comparable in size (14.7 by 7.5 m). Excavations next year will have to clarify its stratigraphic relationship to other Acropolis features, its basic orientation, and even its integrity as a single structure.

Structure 1B-Sub. 2 (Fig. 2:k)

A third buried structure (Str. 1B-Sub.2) was discovered in 1976 west of Str. 1B-Sub.3. Excavations, supervised by Milla-Villeda, revealed the truncated upper zones and vaulting of a building, buried intact up to the middle of the upper zone, with the room filled and the roof removed to form the subsequent flat platform top. Remains of stone corbelled vaulting were found, as were tops of both jambs of an extremely wide north-facing doorway (3.60 m wide). Deep excavation exposed the buried room floor, within the doorway, some four meters beneath the present platform surface. A second floor was found 1.20 m beneath the first, probably corresponding to the level of the building's supporting platform. This lower level is at 71.80 m, or only two meters above the surface of the "zoomorph terrace" in front of the structure. Thus Str. 1B-Sub.2 originally sat on a low platform and faced north on axis with the present location of Monuments 16 and 24.

Str. 1B-Sub.2 is well preserved, even though the walls are too weakened to ever be re-exposed to view. The upper zone was decorated with simple geometric designs achieved by varying the depths of surface planes of the individual building stones. Much of the vault was also preserved.

The building was heavily buttressed during use, first by an abutting platform at the southeast corner, laid against the core of the building walls after the corner masonry had fallen away or had been ripped out. Secondly, a well-built sloping buttress wall about 4 m high was laid around the back, sides and front corners of the building. The buttress formed a single unbroken terrace wall from the building platform to the upper zone, supporting the medial molding but leaving the decorations exposed.

Termination of use for Str. 1B-Sub.2 occurred when the roof was ripped off, the room was filled with crude masonry supporting/retaining walls and masses of river-cobble fill, and cobble fills and terrace facings were laid against all sides of the building and its buttresses. No collapse material was seen on the room floor exposed in the doorway, so the roof had probably not collapsed prior to the filling. Large schist slabs, used as capstones in Quirigua, were thrown into the upper parts of the room fill. Burial of the structure occurred simultaneously with the burial of Str. 1B-Sub.3 and the construction of the great southern stairway of the Ballcourt Plaza (see above). No trace of a structure has been found at the top of this staircase, so the two north-facing structures were never replaced, in contrast to the case of Str. 1B-5-2nd. Possibly a long structure comparable to Str. 1B-17 was planned but never begun.

Deeper excavation next year might be able to determine the stratigraphic relationship between the building and the "zoomorph terrace" even though a direct link to the dates on the monuments might elude us. The four monuments in front of Str. 1B-Sub.2 (Monuments 15, 16, 23 and 24) form a definite group spanning only five to ten years and possibly covering the reign of Ruler II (Kelley 1962). It is possible that Str. 1B-Sub.2 was the focal structure of the group. If so, why was the first monument pair (Monuments 15 and 23) placed neither on its axis nor on that of Str. 1B-Sub.3? Was symmetry to Sub.2 intended with a third monument pair to be placed west of Monument 16? Because of the inaugural motif on the next dated monument (Monument 9), Monument 16 has been thought of as the terminal monument for the reign of Ruler II and might point to a tomb within Str. 1B-Sub.2.

The West Side of the Acropolis

This massive architectural unit, which supports Strs. 1B-3 and 4 (Fig. 2:q,o), was the subject of intensive excavation in 1976. The 1975 east-west center trench was deepened, trenches were begun parallel to it and axial to Strs. 1B-3 and 4, and many smaller lateral trenches were dug at points where the form and stratigraphic relationships of features could be discovered. At present, there can be distinguished two principal stages of growth on the western side of the Acropolis, overlying an earlier unnamed construction about which little is known (see Fig. 3).

The latest construction consists of the final wide large-block stairway (Fig. 3:i) on the east face of the platform (west side of the Acropolis Plaza), along with the walls and floors which cover the earlier platform and its many structures and additions (Fig. 3:h,e,c).

The earlier stage (Fig. 3:g,f) originally had a wide central stairway rising four meters from the level of the Acropolis Plaza (then 2 m lower than in its final form) to a series of three upper terraces, or steps, each over two meters deep and 0.60 m high. The uppermost terrace flooring sustains the free-standing masonry wall (Fig. 3:d; also Fig. 2:p), 23.3 m long and 1.5 m thick, found in 1975. The wall is beautifully decorated on the western side of its upper zone with three torso deity figures identified as *Kinich Ahau*. Excavations in 1976 showed that the wall was centered over the eastern stairway and that no other constructions touched the wall when first built. Visually, then, this wall was the central focus for the platform, but since it stands on the top platform floor, we are not sure whether it was erected at the same time or somewhat later.

The platform stairway is flanked by sloping terrace faces which abut Str. 1B-2 (Fig 2:r). The southern edge of the platform also abuts this structure and was traced back to its southwest corner, where it forms a single sloping terrace over 5 m high, broken only by a projecting apron moulding near its top. The southern part of the platform is wider than the central part—over 23 m wide as opposed to 7 m. It sustained a construction antecedent to and buried by Str. 1B-3. This appears to be another platform, but we know little about either its form or relationship to the free-standing wall on the same supporting platform.

The northern extent of the earlier platform was not confidently determined in 1976, except that it is known to extend beyond the axis of Str. 1B-4. The top surface is about at the same level as that which sustains Str. 1B-5-2nd (see above), and the two might have joined surfaces.

The 1976 excavations established that a sequence of constructions gradually filled up the small courtyard west of the free-standing wall. Constructions under the later Strs. 1B-3 and 4 abutted the ends of the wall and thus formed a courtyard, open to the west. The construction under Str. 1B-4 was a large raised platform with an east stairway on the same axis as the later structure and a south stairway leading up the west side of the wall. The construction under Str. 1B-3 might have been similar but underwent considerable destruction in the building of Str. 1B-3. Filling of the court between these two constructions began when the northern platform and stairway were expanded into the court with the erection of Str. 1B-4; and they were subsequently expanded again (Fig. 3:b). These two operations covered the north half of the wall up to the level of the *Kinich Ahau* figures. Next, the south half of the wall's western face was covered, this time obscuring the

lower half of the figures, including the beautifully carved sun-god face. Next, Str. 1B-3 was built. Then, both halves of the court were raised (Fig. 3:c), probably coincident with the destruction and burial of the top of the free-standing wall and the building of the new stairway and floors of the latest western platform. The southern part of the court was raised about one meter, with what appears to be a narrow north-facing stairway. That these huge fill operations of the courtyard seem to have been undertaken in connection with independent activities in the areas of Strs. 1B-3 and 4 might serve to explain the alternation of constructions in the north and south halves of the court.

Early Constructions

Two early constructions were located under the east stairway of the early western platform. On the axis of the platform is a high wall (Fig. 3:j) rising from the lowermost plaza level and perhaps part of a building, platform, or free-standing wall. In line with the above wall, and on the axis of Str. 1B-3, was found a low bench-like construction, painted red, with a beautifully laid schist-slab paving both on its top and on the floor in front. Both features reflect the later positions of the plaza's western boundary and might be two parts of a single construction.

Structure 1B-4 (Fig. 2:o)

In 1976, the area in front of this structure was cleaned of the backdirt from the old clearing operations, and a long trench was begun axial to the building. A platform underlying the structure has been described above. Directly upon this platform and with the same orientation, axis and general dimensions were built the walls of Str. 1B-4 and a new frontal stairway. The juncture of building and platform was such that the two formed a finished product, and thus we cannot yet be sure whether the subsequent east stairway renewal was part of the structure or a later addition. The stratigraphy is certain, but the lengths of time between constructions are not. On the south, east, and north sides of Str. 1B-4, many additions and buttressing units were built, but some of them over badly cracked and tumbled walls. Inside the building, several wall sections seem to have been replaced, and many secondary features such as benches and an interior stairway to the roof were added. These additions suggest severe structural problems which might have been caused by earthquakes, poor underpinnings or weak wall construction. It is interesting that the floor surface of the platform underlying the structure is also badly slumped and cracked.

Structure 1B-3 (Fig. 2:q)

This structure was investigated by an axial trench in front and in back, by excavations at its juncture with the free-standing wall and by clearing of the southern side.

As mentioned above, Str. 1B-3 was built upon an earlier construction which, like that under Str. 1B-4, anticipated it in several features. A southern stairway underlies a southern side stairway of the structure, and the west and north walls of the platform approximate the equivalent walls of the structure. However, Str. 1B-3 was built into the old construction, thereby destroying much of it.

Although Str. 1B-3 is more solid and much later than Str. 1B-4, and therefore has fewer renovations and additions, large buttresses were also found against its two front corners and walls.

Structure 1B-1 (Fig. 2:s)

The 1975 excavations in front of this structure had uncovered an earlier structure (Fig. 2:t), apparently facing west toward Str. 1B-2, along with a free-standing wall (Fig. 2:u) extending east from the southeast corner of this buried structure. In 1976, the wall was revealed again near its eastern extremity, but further investigation of the entire eastern side of the Acropolis was reserved for the 1977 season. The buried structure was investigated in 1976. It was seen to have been L-shaped and oriented north instead of west. Its position directly across the plaza from Str. 1B-5-2nd and the somewhat similar masonry of these two structures suggest that they might be roughly contemporary. The buried structure, 1B-1-2nd, abuts the wall of Str. 1B-2. However, it is, in turn, abutted by the buttresses of Str. 1B-2, making it very early in the Acropolis sequence, preceding the early western platform with its decorated wall.

Some low masonry walls were investigated on the platform surface at the western end of Str. 1B-1. The walls might be later secondary rooms attached to the main building, composed of one or two stone courses and, presumably, perishable walls and roof.

Structure 1B-6 (Fig. 2v)

In the final weeks of the 1976 season, an axial trench in front of this structure was started. The building is not early, as Morley thought, but built with the uppermost Acropolis Plaza floor. However, an earlier stairway and

an even earlier corner of a pyramid or platform were uncovered, making it clear that the area underwent major renovations. The trench will be continued next year.

Status of the Acropolis Excavations through 1976

The 1976 excavations began to tie together the features discovered in 1975. One of the most interesting possibilities emerging at this date is that the outer faces of the Acropolis went through a construction phase typified by high walls, preceded and followed by phases marked by short terracings and broad stairways. This is best shown in the southwest part of the Acropolis, where the four low terraces of Str. 1B-2 are abutted by the high terrace wall of the earlier western platform and themselves topped by the high steep buttresses against the structure walls. The western edge of the early western platform is also formed by high walls wherever seen. All of these high walls later were covered by low terraces and stairways around the western edge of the Acropolis, from behind Str. 1B-1 to behind Str. 1B-5, effectively transforming the Acropolis from a private and defensible raised plaza to a more accessible one. However, the eastern side of the plaza has yet to be investigated with this hypothesis in mind. If these changes can be documented by further stratigraphic interrelationships, they might suggest important arguments concerning the function of the Quirigua Acropolis—river fort, outpost or rival of Copan, regional capital, or ceremonial center. If the Acropolis was at one time fortified, was it before, during, or after the period of the great stelae? The tentative connection to Monument 16 mentioned above suggests that the constructions covering the high walls occurred during or after the rule of the so-called Ruler II (Kelley 1962), although this has not yet been demonstrated stratigraphically.

Another theme that seems to be emerging from the research at Quirigua is the extent of renovation to existing structures. Almost every platform and building on the Acropolis has additions to it; many were buttresses for corners and walls, others had unknown functions. Buttressing was often patchwork, with the original attempt added to over and over again. The builders of Quirigua also incorporated old architectural features in new constructions. For example, the terrace which flanked the great stairway of the early western platform was renovated simply by building a new facing directly on top of the old one, instead of by obscuring the old terrace. Also, when the south stairway of the Ballcourt Plaza was built, some of the old terraces of Str. 1B-5-1st beside it were retained and extended to fit the new design, rather than ripped out or buried. It is often impossible to detect these renovations in the masonry of the walls themselves, and they are sometimes seen only by excavation within the wall fill.

Thus the stratigraphy of the Acropolis is extremely complex in spite of what seems to be a relatively short period of growth, perhaps as little as a century if the monument associations mentioned above are accepted. Of course, the many changes also provide us with an unusual amount of information from which behavior patterns and adaptations can be inferred.

THE GREAT PLAZA

Several structures on the peripheries of the great stela plaza were investigated this year (see site-core map inside back cover).

Structure 1A-3

The 1975 investigation of this huge mound at the north end of the Great Plaza was reopened in an attempt to find the western end of the partially buried earlier platform. The probe, supervised by Weeks, was based to some degree on the fact that the two early stelae in front of the mound, Monuments 4 (D) and 6 (F), are roughly on axis to the high eastern part of the construction. Thus it was hypothesized that the platform might have been extended to the west at 9.17.0.0.0 when Monument 5 (E) was put up and then capped with its axial summit platform when Monument 7 (G) was placed on axis. The top of the rear wall of the early construction was indeed seen to terminate in a flight of three steps where predicted by the assumption of an early Monument 4/6 axis, but ancient removal of masonry prevented us from demonstrating that the bulk of the early construction ended there as well. The western termination was also sought at the base of the front stairway but without success. Next year a probe might be made on the west end of the mound for a rear corner of the earlier structure. Also, a tunnel started in 1975 on axis to the mound and to Monument 7, with its possible death and accession events, might be reopened and extended in search of the tomb of the great Quirigua ruler, the so-called Cauac Sky.

Structure 1A-11

At the end of the 1976 season, trenches were placed on the south side of this huge pyramid after the mound

had been bushed (supervised by Jones). The base of a southern outset stairway was identified, as were remains of terraces east of the stairway. The other sides are not yet explored and the building has not been penetrated. Further work is planned here during the 1977 season.

Structure 1A-8

After bushing, trenches were placed along the western face of this structure in order to determine its form prior to penetration (the latter tentatively planned for 1977). This work, supervised by Sedat, revealed a central outset stairway and side terraces constructed of large sandstone blocks. Further evidence of masonry robbing was encountered at this location.

Structure 1A-10

The western side of this smaller mound was also bushed and investigated under the supervision of Sedat. The northwest corner terraces were found in good condition, but many of the stones of the outset stairway had been ripped out. An axial trench was started into the cobble fill and is slated for continuation next year. A low frontal terrace, extending several meters to the west, was suggested by magnetometer survey (see below) and confirmed by excavation.

Magnetometer Survey

A brief magnetometer survey was conducted within the Great Plaza and the Ballcourt Plaza in order to determine if buried constructions and monuments might be detectable. The search for buried monuments was unsuccessful, but since sandstone and rhyolite are not highly magnetic, it still remains possible that buried monuments exist at Quirigua. Another means of locating them would have to be found in order to test this possibility. The attempt to locate buried construction was more successful; a pavement and terrace mapped by magnetometer west of Str. 1A-10 (see above) reinforced the idea that the massive Great Plaza may be composed of separate pavement units, rather than being a single continuous construction. This possibility must be tested during subsequent seasons.

SITE-PERIPHERY PROGRAM

Site-periphery research in 1976 again comprised both survey and excavation. Supplemental support from the National Science Foundation (BNS7603283) allowed expansion of survey techniques this season to include magnetic mapping and air reconnaissance, as well as the more traditional foot survey. The goals of the program this season were to complete identification, mapping and surface collection of prehistoric activity loci outside the site-core and to begin test excavations in a sample of these loci.

SURVEY PROGRAM

Foot Survey

Walking reconnaissance was carried out from January 27 through March 27 by Ashmore, Milla-Villeda and Schortman. During this period over 80 new prehistoric activity loci were discovered in an area of some 95 km², with surface collections taken whenever possible. Most of these collections were sparse and the sherds eroded; two conspicuous exceptions (Loci 086 and 087) were identified in recently plowed and sown and, in one case, looted, milpa sites. Of the 56 architectural-group loci, 37 were mapped at 1:1000 scale by Brunton compass and steel tape, with two large groups recorded at the same scale by transit.

Primary attention was focused on the Chapulco plain (see Fig. 1), a previously unsurveyed territory reputed to contain abundant evidence of precolumbian occupation. Thirty-five loci were recorded in the area bounded by Switch Molina and Finca La Marina on the west, the Motagua River on the north, the Morja River on the east, and the Jubuco River on the south.

North of the Motagua, strip surveys were conducted —between Finca El Pilar and the Atlantic Highway (at Guacamayo), between the highway (about 3 km northeast of Guacamayo) and ca. 1.25 km north of the San Francisco River, and between the highway (about 2.5 km northeast of Guacamayo) and the Mejia Canal—to expand our knowledge of settlement on the valley terraces above the alluvial plain. This work yielded 8 new activity loci beyond the 16 recorded farther southwest last season.

On the plain itself, intensive survey around the Quirigua site-core was essentially completed this year, with at least a kilometer radius in all directions having been investigated. In addition, the Mejia Canal—which runs northeast about one kilometer north of the site-core—was bushed and examined along its banks for a distance of about 1.5 km from its intersection of the site access road, yielding 1 structure and a rich Late Classic midden. In all, 40 activity loci were added to the 14 recorded on the Quirigua plain in 1975.

Magnetometer Survey

Using a cesium magnetometer, Bruce Bevan of the Museum Applied Science Center for Archaeology, University Museum, spent approximately one month attempting to locate buried precolumbian remains. It was hoped that this work would reveal low platforms and other small remains obscured by the alluvium which now covers the entire valley floor to a depth of 0.60 m or more. Although several construction features were located, in general interpretation of magnetic contours was complicated by the combination of low overall magnetic properties of ancient construction materials and broad distribution of modern iron debris from agricultural machinery.

Specific results of the magnetometer survey are as follows: A 30 m wide transect due east, from the "East Group" (Strs. 1B-14 through 1B-16) to the canal lying a kilometer away, the west bank of which was examined as Locus 032 in 1975, yielded eight indications for possible testing in 1977; most of this area, however, was devoid of archaeologically promising magnetic anomalies. A similar transect northwest of the site-core, between Loci 004 (a possible ballcourt) and 006 (open plaza group tested by excavation in 1975) produced similar results (see below). Perhaps the most successful application of magnetometer survey was the location and preliminary tracing of a possible causeway feature. Originally found as three contiguous stones in a posthole being dug for a new section of park fence, the "causeway" appeared in magnetic mapping as a series of magnetic anomalies running approximately 95° east of north. Since the source of the magnetic anomalies was fill material—a small, apparently randomly distributed portion of the fill stones—the line was not continuous; nonetheless it has apparently been detected for a distance of ca. 90 m east of the original discovery point and may have been found in the transect between Loci 004 and 006. Preliminary tests of the causeway feature were begun this year (see below) and will be continued in 1977. The brief magnetometer survey within the site-core is reported above, and a more detailed account of magnetometer work as a whole will be published as a separate *Quirigua Paper*.

Air Survey

Using a single-engine Cessna with the passenger's door removed, Ashmore and Schortman made a rapid air reconnaissance of the Quirigua area in the late afternoon of March 29 and the early morning of March 30. On the latter flight they were accompanied by Bevan and Glavis, to assist with photography. Over 300 photographs (both black-and-white and color) were taken of various loci; these are all oblique shots. Infrared film was also tested but did not reveal any features beyond those recorded with conventional film. The area covered is a rough quadrilateral with approximate corners at La Pita (NW), Cristina (NE), Mixco (SE) and Finca La Marina (SW) and included all areas surveyed on foot (see Fig. 1).

Two previously unknown loci were discovered near the Jubuco River between Las Vinas and Finca Nueva (see Fig. 1); none new were discovered north of the Motagua. Thus, even though special effort was made to scan previously unexamined areas and studied areas where no remains had been found, the air survey basically confirmed the results of the foot survey. It is still possible that some small remains have been missed since several known mounds less than 1 m high could not be seen from the air, but the air reconnaissance gives us confidence that the patterns described below are fairly accurate.

Table 1

DISTRIBUTION OF LOCI BY FORM AND LOCATION

	Chapulco Plain	Quirigua Plain	Uplands north of Motagua	Totals
Non-architectural loci	11	38	8	57
Single mounds and small irregular groups	10	8	11	29
Small regularly arranged groups	10°	6°°	2	18
Quadrangles	2	1	0	3
Special/complex loci	2	1°°°	3	6
Totals	35	54	24	113

° Includes 2 possible ballcourts

°° Includes 1 possible ballcourt

°°° Not including site-core (Quirigua Park)

Summary of Survey Findings

In two seasons of survey 113 loci have been identified beyond the limits of the site-core. A rough preliminary taxonomy by form has been set up, and the distribution of loci by formal category and by location is shown in Table 1; in specifying locations, more attention has been paid to spatial and geographical aspects than to ecological ones. The formal categories are only tentative but match well both with the general complexity continuum one would expect and with the specific continuum noted elsewhere in the lower Motagua valley by Nowak.

Non-architectural loci include primarily surface sherd scatters, but also one midden; of course, subsequent excavation might reveal buried construction. Small irregular groups have provisionally been classed with single mounds (presumably architectural platforms) representing the least "arranged," and probably often partly destroyed, architectural remains. Small, regularly arranged groups include three presumed ballcourts and small open plazuelas (i.e. courts bounded on at least two sides by platforms). Quadrangles are like plazuelas but are bounded on at least three sides and are larger in all dimensions, with access to the central court more restricted than in the smaller groups.

That is, the court is closed on two or more corners. The final category shows no formal consistency among its constituents; these loci are temporarily segregated as a unit for "special/complex" characteristics such as unusually large size (e.g., Locus 092) or the presence of stone monuments (e.g., Locus 002). Admittedly all the classes are very loosely defined, but for the purposes of this preliminary report, and to stress the initial nature of the classification, the present definitions are felt to be adequate.

Bearing in mind the provisional and non-excavational (i.e., non-functional) status of this classification, one can nonetheless postulate therefrom a social continuum, with lower status or less centralized functions associated with loci at the upper end of the table (and vice versa). Spatial distribution of the loci accords with this hypothesis and with a central-place model of settlement. That is, *all* loci tend to be located on slight to marked rises or precipices, near water sources and modern trails; deliberate search in areas not so characterized yielded no loci. But quadrangles and "special" loci tend to be spaced in a way that suggests they are local power nodes (administrative, economic, etc.) in a hierarchical system with Quirigua at the head. These higher-order units are at least 2 km apart, and the most extensive and complex loci outside of the core area are also farthest from it (i.e., Loci 024, 057 and 092). They are also located in positions strategic for control of trade and access, such as the points where upland river valleys open onto the alluvial plain. Group A (Locus 002) is visible from virtually all these loci—and from Quirigua—and may have served as a relay signalling station. The location of Quirigua itself is the approximate point of convergence of lines projected from the mouths of several of these river valleys (e.g., the Motagua, Morja and Jubuco). At present these functional characterizations are untested inferences, but they provide a set of directions for the 1977 excavations.

Fuller chronological data will also be pursued in 1977. A series of Late Preclassic figurine heads and a chert tanged large blade were recorded, although their exact provenience is unknown since they were found by local inhabitants. Nothing else was noted, either in the field or during initial laboratory examinations, which would surely indicate occupation in other than Late Classic/Early Postclassic times. That is, surface collections have yielded no evidence to refute a model of late and brief occupation for this part of the lower Motagua valley. The sporadic Preclassic finds argue for an earlier occupation, but not necessarily for continuity of occupation between that time and the end of the

Classic. (See below concerning Preclassic/Protoclassic materials from the excavations in Locus 029.)

An interesting pattern has been noted in that the architectural loci immediately north of the site-core seem to fall in a rough east-west band, aligned toward Group A on a ridge to the northwest. Constituent elements of the band include "Group B" (Locus 025, a "special" locus, or plazuela plus monument) on the west, Loci 072, (plazuela), 006 (plazuela), 029 (later shown to be a plazuela), 004 (ballcourt), 082 (quadrangle), and 026 (plazuela), the series spanning approximately 2 km and running slightly south of east. The 95° orientation of the "causeway" is comparable, and further probes in 1977 will test the hypothesis that the "causeway" served to link these loci.

EXCAVATION

Excavation as part of site-periphery research comprised ceramic test-pitting, tests of the "causeway," and extensive excavations in two architectural groups.

Ceramic Test-Pitting

Two sets of tests were done to gather stratified ceramic samples from the site-periphery. The first was an attempt to relocate a possible midden discovered by Nowak in 1974 within the confines of the laboratory compound. The apparent midden was encountered, but whereas Nowak apparently hit close to its center, our 2 x 2 m pit seems to have been near an edge: we retrieved only one bag of sherds from the 20-cm level at which Nowak found seven full bags. Sherds above and below were sparse and excavation was discontinued with the level that yielded only two sherds (1.80 to 2.00 m below surface).

The other set of ceramic tests was a series of three pits near the center of three of the surface concentrations recorded last year as Locus 032. Although these finds had been in modern canal backdirt, we assumed the backdirt came from approximately adjacent to its present position, and we hoped to get a reversed stratigraphic sample overlying the undisturbed sample. All three excavations were disappointing in terms of ceramic quantity—only 1 lot of the 26 yielded more than a dozen sherds—but were continued until the water table was reached, at variable depths between 1.90 to 2.60 m below surface. The southernmost of the three excavations did yield several lumps of adobe between 0.60 and 1.60 m, hinting at possible construction in the vicinity.

Causeway Tests

Villa Rojas (1934) noted that Morley had told him of a "causeway" encountered by the United Fruit Company when the latter was building its railroad in 1910-1912. The feature was said to lie a meter below the surface, heading toward "some unknown point to the northeast". This meagre description was enough to suggest that the three stones found in a posthole (see section on magnetometer survey, above), some 0.63 m below surface, near the company railroad line and northeast of the site-core, might represent the reputed causeway. Magnetometer mapping indicated strong anomalies, but running in an east-west, rather than the expected northeast-southwest, direction. A pit was positioned over the strongest anomaly, and although we thought we might find only buried iron (railroad debris), we encountered instead the south edge of a pavement of large schist slabs—one of which had been notched to fit—overlying a shallow bed (ca. 0.30 m) of cobble fill. As this pit already intruded on the Del Monte Fruit Company's access road, we could not expand it to section the feature, so a new pit was begun east of the first and within the limits of the park. The paved alignment was encountered at the same depth, but here the fill was uneven, ca. 0.30 m deep in the western part of the pit, and 1.35 m deep in the eastern part. In the latter section, the fill was also stratigraphically differentiable: cobbles set "flat" in the basal half, overlain by a mix of rough rhyolite and sandstone chunks, which were in turn capped by the paving slabs. There was no other discontinuity of construction evident where the fill depth plunged so suddenly, and it seems to represent simply a levelling operation at the time of construction. Sherds were sparse throughout, and nonexistent below basal construction.

Another set of causeway excavations, in the field adjacent to the east edge of the park, was designed to give a somewhat more distant third point for establishing the causeway alignment and to allow a full cross-section cut where there was no danger of intersecting the modern access road (cf. Locus 029, below, for final causeway tests). Unfortunately two pits, located at indicated magnetic anomalies, yielded no construction features and only a handful of sherds, all of which were from one pit. Hoping the failure here was due simply to inaccurate pit placement relative to the anomalies, we will resume work in 1977 to trace and section this construction feature. This season's excavation demonstrated the existence of a low pavement of unknown length and width; whether it is truly a "causeway" or not

and, if so, where it goes, are questions that must await the new season to be answered.

Architectural Groups

Excavations began April 1 in one irregularly arranged group (Locus 029) and one plazuela (Locus 026), both on the alluvial plain north of the river. Each was selected randomly to represent its locus class (see Table 1 and Fig. 1), and each was originally to be tested by two 2 x 2 m pits designed to penetrate axially one presumed structure (seeking constructional, functional and dating information) and to locate a possible midden off the corner of that "structure." These excavations were later expanded to examine the overall loci more extensively, and work continued until April 24, the end of the season.

Locus 029. Located in 1975, this group was originally mapped as three irregularly oriented structures. Structure 3C-1 (in the Quirigua designation system), the easternmost, is ca. 0.70 m high and rectangular in shape; the central structure, 3C-2, ca. 0.84 m high and oriented roughly north-south, is rectangular with a lower platform projecting to the north; Str. 3C-3, ca. 0.75 m high, is rather amorphous in plan and is situated to the west. Excavations in 1976 concentrated on Strs. 3C-1 and 3C-2 (supervised by Schortman).

The principal work in Str. 3C-1 consisted of a 1-m-wide trench designed to bisect the structure, with shallower trenches used to locate the southwest and southeast corners. These excavations revealed a single-component construction of cobble fill with a hearting of mixed stone and earth, about 14.9 m long on its main, east-west axis. Very little cut masonry was found *in situ* although several fallen blocks were encountered nearby. On the south, the basal terrace rises ca. 0.62 m above the inferred original ground surface. It was constructed of a combination of cobbles and faced sandstone blocks and rests on a crushed rhyolite floor. The upper south-facing terrace, 0.30 m high, lies about 1.60 m north of the lower and was built entirely of tightly packed cobbles. Presumably this terrace as well was once faced with cut masonry though no such stones were found in place. The northern or "rear" terrace facing rises directly to a level equivalent to the upper southern terrace; it is composed of a combination of cobbles and cut sandstone blocks. The masonry in this terrace, however, does not appear as formal as that noted in the basal southern terrace, nor does this feature rest on any discernible prepared floor. The lines of two cobble fill-retaining walls, one each 0.70-0.90 m inside the faces of the outermost terraces, were also noted during the course of excavation. In addition to these features, the axial trench exposed, in section, the remains of two parallel walls located on the summit of the structure. These walls of faced rhyolite blocks represent either the uppermost terrace of the substructure or the foundations of a superstructure, now largely destroyed or robbed. No evidence for flooring of any kind was noted. Finally, the metate and mano located near the northern basal terrace line suggest that Str. 3C-1 served as a residence, although, admittedly, evidence supporting this supposition is minimal.

The work carried out on Str. 3C-2 focused on two areas. In the first, an axial trench revealed no evidence of construction of either stone or earth except for a buried stone chamber. This chamber, located at the approximate center of the mound, ca. 0.68 m below the summit surface, had walls of roughly faced sandstone blocks and was roofed by a double layer of transversely laid schist slabs. The chamber measured about 2.40 m east-west by 1.0 m north-south and was 0.50 m deep. Although in both form and construction it resembled the burial crypts of the San Agustin Acasaguastlan area (Smith and Kidder 1943), its only contents were three complete pottery vessels clustered at the eastern end of the schist-slab floor. Two of these vessels were large hemispherical bowls, apparently corresponding to the Late or Terminal Classic. The third, a low, cylindrical tetrapod 15 cm in diameter, while of the same type as the first two, showed some attributes reminiscent of the Early or Middle Classic. Excavations were continued to about 0.90 m below the level of the chamber floor, but no further deposits and only one sherd were encountered.

The second focus of activity at Str. 3C-2 was a pit on the northeast corner of the previously mentioned low projecting platform. Within 0.17 m of ground surface, a cobble pavement was encountered, usually one cobble thick and underlain by what appeared to be undifferentiated earth fill. To the south the pavement was followed for ca. 3.66 m, where it ended in a line of roughly faced sandstone blocks. About 1.31 m farther south an east-west wall composed of two courses of cut sandstone blocks was located but could not be fully cleared in the time available. Establishing contemporaneity between the pavement and this wall is hampered by the lack of any definite, formal flooring linking the two, but the similarity in elevation of these two features and the existence of what appears to be a debris line stretching from the base of the pavement to just beneath the upper course of the wall may argue for some degree of contemporaneity.

About 1.0 m below the upper pavement, in the northwest corner of this excavation, another concentration of cobbles was discovered. This surface, too, was only one cobble, or ca. 0.08 m thick. Its special significance is that, whereas ceramics from the upper levels of this pit suggest Terminal Classic occupation, the materials both immediately above and for approximately 1.15 m below the lower cobble surface appear to date to the Late or Terminal Preclassic. The material from these levels, if future more detailed analyses support the initial assessment, represents the first excavated sample of Preclassic artifacts from the immediate Quirigua area. The lack of surface indications of such early occupation underscores both the local severity of the problem of alluvial "masking" and the unreliability of surface collections as predictors of subsurface deposits.

The features encountered in and adjacent to Str. 3C-2 (the upper cobble pavement and wall noted above, and the axial buried chamber) lack good stratigraphic links. Until further excavations are carried out, however, preliminary ceramic analysis places all of them in the Terminal Classic, and they may, therefore, represent a single architectural complex. One possible reconstruction of such a complex would show a low cobble-surfaced platform projecting north from a low, sandstone wall. The wall might extend farther (east-west) than the platform and then south to circumscribe the previously noted chamber. The chamber seems to have been intentionally buried by an earth mound with no formal superstructure subsequently built over it. Functionally, the little evidence on hand suggests that this structure and, in particular, the chamber it contains were used in some form of ritual activity.

Contemporaneity of Strs. 3C-1 and 3C-2 is assumed, but, due to the apparent lack of a continuous pavement between the two, stratigraphic demonstration of this point seems precluded.

In addition to the above excavations, two pits were dug about 53.0 m and 53.5 m to the southeast of Locus 029 in what appeared to be an area devoid of prehistoric activity. The purpose of these excavations was to determine if any hidden activity loci might be situated in these "vacant areas" and, more specifically, to see if the previously described causeway might be intersected. The results on both points were negative.

In sum, Locus 029 appears to have been occupied at roughly the same time as the site-core of Quirigua; to have served as a focus for both residential and ceremonial activity; and to have involved several different constructional techniques. Further excavations in this group will serve to test the validity of the above assessments and to enlarge our understanding of the dating, constructional techniques, and activities relevent to this group.

Locus 026. Originally located in 1975, this group has an open plaza arrangement: a large mound, Str. 2C-1, ca. 2.5 m high, on the north; a barely perceptible mound, Str. 2C-2, on the west; and a mound about 0.65 m high, Str. 2C-3, on the east, with a projection from the south end of Str. 2C-3 closing off the south side of the central court.

The principal excavations focused on Str. 2C-3 (supervised by Ashmore). There, axial trenching and expanded lateral excavations revealed a single-component construction of mud fill overlain by cobble and sandstone/rhyolite fill-retaining walls (on the rear only), and faced with sandstone masonry. The structure was badly ruined on all but the west (front) face, and therefore the original plan is not fully known. Many construction features are slumped, probably due to erosional loss of supporting mud fill.

A pavement of schist slabs runs along the entire west face of the structure, extending from it a maximum of 2.6 m. Laid partially on and partially adjacent to this pavement, a single sandstone step leads up to the supporting platform of the structure. This platform is now 14 m north-south, a length probably close to the original maximum for the structure.

Only the south jamb of the central doorway was exposed, and the front wall of the structure was followed from there to an abrupt (non-corner) end 3.6 m to the south. Just south of this point there is evidence of an eastward continuation of the schist surface of the frontal platform, implying that the original corner of the front wall was not much farther south than its present non-corner end.

The schist "flooring" just noted runs under the front wall and, in the doorway, continues into the structure as far as does the eastward extension of the doorjamb. There was a layer of cobbles extending about 0.25 m east of the slabs in the north portion of the axial pit; perhaps this was part of a rough, unplastered "floor." Another sandstone-block wall, or bench front, was encountered 0.20 m to the east, but it lacked a stratigraphic link with the "floor." This interior (west-facing) wall did not even reach the south wall of the axial trench, and this fact plus the lack of masonry continuation from the doorjamb make determination of room form difficult. Not even a rough wall was found continuing east of the extant limit of doorjamb masonry, while a solidly packed construction unit of

cobbles ran south; since it would have faced only the room's interior, perhaps this cobble unit formed the (once plastered?) wall. Fragments of adobe (burnt clay in amorphous lumps) were found axially throughout the collapsed debris above the floor, in distributions suggesting they were part of somewhat-less-substantially-constructed upper portions of the original superstructure; no impressions, such as of other construction elements, were noted. A line of tumbled masonry on the rear of the structure indicates that the ruined east edge of the platform was probably less than 7.5 m east of its front edge. It is possible that this represents a "false-front" structure similar to those described for Cozumel (Sabloff and Rathje 1975). Such an appearance, however, might here be due to differential erosion, the rear and sides of the structure being more exposed to flooding and therefore more prone than the front to being washed away.

A single extended human burial of an adult female, probably in her mid-20's, was encountered on the axis of the structure. The burial pit had been cut through the floor—even through the stone-slab portion— in front (west) of the interior wall, and was of minimum dimensions to accommodate its occupant. It is not clear whether a new floor was laid after the interment.

Although no certain mortuary goods were found in the pit, sherds, charcoal and schist chips, the latter presumably from the cut slab, were distributed throughout the fill, and a small celt (serpentine?) was found near the top of the pit. Six button-like discs of oxidized copper, perhaps attached to a cloak or shroud, were found on the skeleton.

Evidence is minimal, but Str. 2C-3 was most likely a residence. Burial beneath the house floor fits common Maya practice. And pieces of one or more broken metates as well as several broken *ollas* (cooking pots) or parts thereof were found on or above the pavements/floors. More detailed artifactual and ceramic analyses are pending. Dating is likely Terminal Classic, based on field assessment of ceramics, or Early Postclassic, as inferred from the presence of copper in the burial.

Contemporaneity of Strs. 2C-1 and 2C-3 has been provisionally assumed. Due to apparent lack of a continuous court surfacing between the two, stratigraphic demonstration of contemporaneity may be impossible.

Str. 2C-1 was tested by axial clearing, not penetration, of its south face. A broad sandstone staircase, robbed, or just ruined, was recorded in profile, but its exact lateral dimensions as well as internal constructional features will not be known until further work is pursued in 1977. The overburden of debris on the stairs was rich in sherds and censer fragments and included as well a large turbaned figurine head (similar to a smaller one found in a plazuela site on the Chapulco plain), a vessel part shaped like a cacao pod, and at least one eroded sherd of Copador pottery. This structure holds much promise for continued investigation.

In sum, Locus 026 appears at this point to have been at least partially residential (Str. 2C-3) with some elite ceremonial/administrative functions (Str. 2C-1) suggested as well. Its location implies that it may have served as the eastern terminus of the "causeway," but the behavioral ramifications of that position are not, at present, understood, and indeed the actual connection to the "causeway" is not yet demonstrated.

MONUMENT PRESERVATION AND RECORDING PROGRAM

This program has two fundamental objectives—to insure the preservation of the Quirigua monuments and to prepare accurate 1:10-scale line drawings of all monuments and inscriptions at Quirigua. The first objective will be pursued in several stages: the eradication of the threatening botanical growths, the consolidation of the stone, and ultimately, continued maintenance procedures. The first stage was initiated in 1975 by Dr. Mason Hale with the collection and identification of the microfloral species and recommendations as to their destruction (see *Quirigua Paper, No.3*). Hale also tested various biocidal treatments at that time, and during the 1976 season returned to assess the results of their application. Based upon these tests, full-scale spraying of all monuments was begun to destroy the microflora. A solution of borax and chlorox was found to be the safest and most effective treatment. Accordingly, Monuments 2, 8, 9 11, 13, 14, 16 and 24 received an application of this solution during the field season, and the remaining monuments were treated in July 1976. Plans call for periodic applications over the next two or three years to completely destroy all the growths. The local Park maintenance staff can be trained to apply the spray. Subsequently, applications at greater intervals should serve to permanently retard microfloral recolonization.

At the close of the 1976 season experiments were undertaken to assess the promise of a new stone preservative compound developed by Dr. Darrel Butterbaugh of MASCA. Sample blocks of sandstone (the same material as the monuments) were treated with this compound. The effects of the treatment will be observed over the next few years under varying conditions at the site (abundant sunlight, prevalent shade, and conditions of high and low humidity). If the compound proves successful, and pending approval by the Instituto de Antropologia e Historia, it may be applied to the monuments.

The recording of the Quirigua monuments is being pursued through photography (daylight and nighttime), molds and rubbings. Previous work, including Maudslay's photographs, drawings and the various casts (in San Diego, New York, Cambridge and London), will be combined with the present efforts in order to produce the most complete and accurate record possible. During the 1976 season priority was given to recording those monuments that have been poorly recorded in the past, or to those that are most threatened with loss of detail due to erosion and other agents of destruction. Monument 13 (Altar M), containing what is apparently the earliest inscription at Quirigua, was delicately cleaned and photographed. The inscription was then molded with latex, and the resultant cast was photographed and a rubbing prepared. The original inscription was further photographed using artificial light (night photography). Similar procedures were used to record Monuments 17 and 18 (Altars Q and R) and the full-figure glyphs of Monument 2 (Zoomorph B), although no casts have yet been made. Latex molds were, however, made of the full-figure glyphs of Monuments 4 (Stela D, east side) and 23 (Altar of Zoomorph O).

The 17 *in-situ* hieroglyphic blocks of the benches of Str. 1B-1 were cleaned and photographed. A total of 46 hieroglyphic blocks from the upper facade of this structure, found loose about the flanks of this platform, have been collected, cleaned, photographed and stockpiled under protective cover. In addition, a total of 380 miscellaneous carved stones (most or all from fallen decorative facades) have been collected, cleaned and photographed: 110 from the vicinity of Str. 1B-1, 208 from 1B-2, 62 from the area of 1B-3 and 1B-4.

POTTERY ANALYSIS PROGRAM

The pottery collections recovered from the excavations and surface surveys of the Quirigua Project are being subjected to a combined typological and form analysis. This analysis, following the preliminary efforts begun in 1975, was fully developed by Bullard and Sharer during the 1976 season. The approach uses both the type-variety-mode method (Smith, Willey and

Gifford 1960; Gifford 1976) and a vessel form classification. The type-variety-mode approach is based upon the usual criteria—attributes of vessel treatment, color, decoration and other surface characteristics. The form classification is based upon component shape attributes (lip, neck, body, base) and defines a series of overall vessel forms (classed as bowls, jars and other forms).

The form classification currently includes 14 defined vessel shapes. By the end of the 1976 season a total of 51 type-variety units had been isolated and were in the process of being defined. Another ten units are now designated "specials" or potential types without (thus far) adequate numerical representation to allow complete definition.

Using both these classifications, the sherd content of selected lots was examined and recorded according to type-variety content and distributed via the basic vessel form categories. The 62 provenience lots examined in this way in 1976 represent both excavated and surface contexts, from the site-core and its peripheries: with only minor exceptions, the typological content of all these lots was essentially the same. The exceptions, including several lots from Str. 1B-8 (South Group), may represent specialized functional distinctions or temporal differences. Based upon the overall similarities in typological content, a single ceramic complex, as yet unnamed, has been defined at Quirigua. The temporal position of this complex is tentative but appears to correspond to the Late and Terminal Classic, with continuities into the Early Postclassic (ca. A.D. 700-1000). As reported in a preliminary finding from the previous season (see *Quirigua Paper, No. 2*), no tradition of polychrome pottery has been identified to date at Quirigua. Only two or three sherds of Copador pottery, along with a few individual specimens of other (unidentified) polychrome types, have been recovered after two full seasons of excavation.

A preliminary definition of the type-variety-mode content of the Quirigua ceramic complex can be summarized according to its major (frequent) and minor (infrequent) wares, along with a few of the modes identified to date:

Major Wares

fine paste ware (ca. 15 type-variety units, representing monochrome, bichrome, trichrome, fluted, grooved and incised vessels).
coarse orange ware (ca. 4 type-variety units, representing monochrome, bichrome vessels and incised/excised vessels).

Minor Wares

Plumbate ware
talc slip/paste ware
black-brown ware
hematite red ware

Modes

(restricted to those apparently diagnostic of Terminal Classic/Early Postclassic Period)

bell-shaped hollow tripod supports
animal effigy tripod supports
talc-slipped vessels
restricted tall-cylindrical vases

A preliminary observation may be made regarding differential distribution of vessel forms between lots (both excavated and surface proveniences) from the site-core and those from the site-periphery, based upon work completed in 1976. The distribution of the vessel form categories is summarized in Table 2. The site-core sample includes lots from the Ballcourt Plaza and two of its flanking platforms, from the northern Acropolis platform and from Str. 1A-2. Preliminary assessment indicates that most or all of these lots are from secondary contexts (construction-fill debris). Two lots from the base of the early Acropolis western platform appear to represent a primary context; the vessel form distribution from these two lots is anomalous when compared to other site-core lots in the sample. The distribution pattern is similar to that associated with the sample of site-periphery lots and may indicate that ancient activity associated with the early western platform was similar to that typical of peripheral areas.

The differential distribution for vessel forms between the core and peripheries of the site may be summarized as follows (see Table 2). The site-core sample (excluding the two early lots mentioned above) of bowl forms ranges from 24 to 46%, jars from 9 to 23% and censers from 15 to 66%. The site-periphery sample of bowls ranges from 22 to 69%, jars from 28 to 73% and censers from 3 to 5%. Although the bowl category shows an overlapping distribution, perhaps reflective of the diversity of functions associated with bowl forms, the percentage ranges of jars and censers are mutually exclusive between the two provenience categories in this sample. This may reflect an expected distinction in ancient activities between the site-core and its peripheries—a prevalence of censer forms, associated with elite/ritual activities, in the site-core, and a prevalence of jars, associated with non-elite/domestic activities, in the peripheries. It should be emphasized that these data are only preliminary. As the sample of analyzed lots grows in size and diversity in subsequent seasons, we expect a more refined and complex pattern of functional differentiation to emerge. Increased control over temporal and contextual variables will be essential to such a refined study, since the present sample combines lots that represent different contexts, and probably different time spans as well.

The 1976 pottery analysis leads to a preliminary interpretation of continuity in domestic and ceremonial occupation at Quirigua into the Early Postclassic era. This tentative finding appears to have a measure of support from other evidence gathered at Quirigua to date. For instance, there was substantial constructional activity in the Acropolis after the latest Initial Series

date (9.19.0.0.0; A.D. 810) associated with Str. 1B-1. Furthermore, there is considerable evidence of the "robbing" of masonry from outlying structures, presumably for construction efforts during a very late period of occupation. The recovery of metal artifacts from a burial in an outlying group (Str. 2C-3, Locus 026) together with probable Postclassic sherds associated with Str. 1B-8 (South Group) may be indications of Postclassic occupation.

A deposit of Late or Terminal Preclassic pottery was discovered at the close of the season in Locus 029, northwest of the site-core. Time permitted only brief examination of this material; detailed analysis of the lots from this deposit will be undertaken next season. Aside from occasional surface finds, however, this evidence does provide the best indication of Preclassic occupation in the vicinity of Quirigua discovered to date.

Table 2

DISTRIBUTION OF MAJOR FORM CLASSES BY SELECTED PROVENIENCES

Provenience (Structures and Site Areas)	Bowls No. %		Jars No. %		Others No. %		Censers No. %		Total No.
Ballcourt Plaza (southern staircase)	108	27%	76	19%	21	05%	197	49%	402
Ballcourt Plaza (eastern staircase)	436	35%	281	23%	3	-	497	41%	1217
Structure 1A-2	665	46%	319	22%	229	16%	218	15%	1431
Acropolis western platform°	67	74%	19	21%	1	01%	4	04%	91
Acropolis northern platform	314	24%	112	09%	17	01%	852	66%	1295
Structure 1B-8 (south group)	106	48%	98	45%	5	02%	11	05%	220
Locus 006	27	69%	11	28%	0	-	1	03%	39
Locus 086	66	22%	218	73%	0	-	14	05%	298
Locus 087	79	40%	104	53%	5	02%	10	05%	198

°Two lots from the earliest probable primary
context (non-construction fill) yet found in the Acropolis

CONCLUSIONS

The research conducted at Quirigua during the 1976 season represents the continuation of programs initiated during previous years but also includes excavations within previously untested structures. As a result of this work, we feel confident that the original research goals of the Quirigua Project can be met in the remaining two field seasons as planned. Specifically, the site-core program has nearly finished the deep axial trenches on the south and west sides of the Acropolis; the north axial trench (Str. 1B-5) is completed. This work, together with the greatly expanded lateral excavations, has resulted in a preliminary understanding of the sequence of constructional activity in the Quirigua Acropolis. Further investigations are needed, especially to document constructional sequences on the east side of the Acropolis, to further develop linkages between architecture and monuments, and to begin to document ancient activities associated with the Acropolis.

Excavations within Structures 1A-3, 1A-8, 1A-10 and 1A-11 have provided data bearing upon constructional methods and sequences outside the Acropolis, but further work is needed to document the relationships of these structures to the Great Plaza that they flank, as well as to elucidate their ancient functions.

The site-periphery program has completed the task of identifying and mapping ancient activity areas outside the site-core, and the excavation of a stratified sample of these sites was begun in 1976. Continued work is needed in the excavation of peripheral structures in order to determine the temporal and functional range within these areas.

The Quirigua monuments are successfully undergoing treatment designed to destroy the threatening microflora that covers most of their exposed surfaces. This program is to continue, concurrent with experiments to determine effective means of preserving the monuments against further erosion. Three of the least-known monuments at Quirigua were recorded during 1976, using a combination of photography, latex molds and rubbings. This program and allied epigraphic studies are expected to accelerate during subsequent seasons.

The analysis of pottery from Quirigua made substantial progress during 1976, through the development of a combined typological and form classification. This work will continue in order to refine our means of assessing both temporal and functional dimensions of the Quirigua data. Similar work will be initiated in the future for other artifactual and constructional material from the site.

REFERENCES CITED

Gifford, J.C.
  1976 Prehistoric Pottery Analysis and the Ceramics of Barton Ramie in the Belize Valley. Memoirs of the Peabody Museum, Vol. 18. Cambridge:Harvard University.

Kelley, D. H.
  1962 Glyphic Evidence for a Dynastic Sequence at Quirigua, Guatemala. American Antiquity 27: 323-335.

Morley, S. G.
  1935 Guide Book to the Ruins of Quirigua. Carnegie Institution of Washington, Supplementary Publication 16, Washington, D.C.

Nowak, T. R.
  1973 The Lower Motagua Valley Survey Project: First Preliminary Report. Manuscript, American Section, University Museum, University of Pennsylvania.

Sabloff, J. A. and W. L. Rathje
  1975 The Rise of the Maya Merchant Class. Scientific American 233 (4): 72-82.

Smith, A. L. and A. V. Kidder
  1943 Explorations in the Motagua Valley, Guatemala. Carnegie Institution of Washington, Publication 546, Contribution 41, Washington, D.C.

Smith, R. E., G. R. Willey and J. C. Gifford
  1960 The Type-Variety Concept as a Basis for the Analysis of Maya Pottery. American Antiquity 25: 330-340.

Villa Rojas, A.
  1934 The Yaxuna-Coba Causeway. Carnegie Institution of Washington, Publication 436, Contribution 9, Washington, D.C.

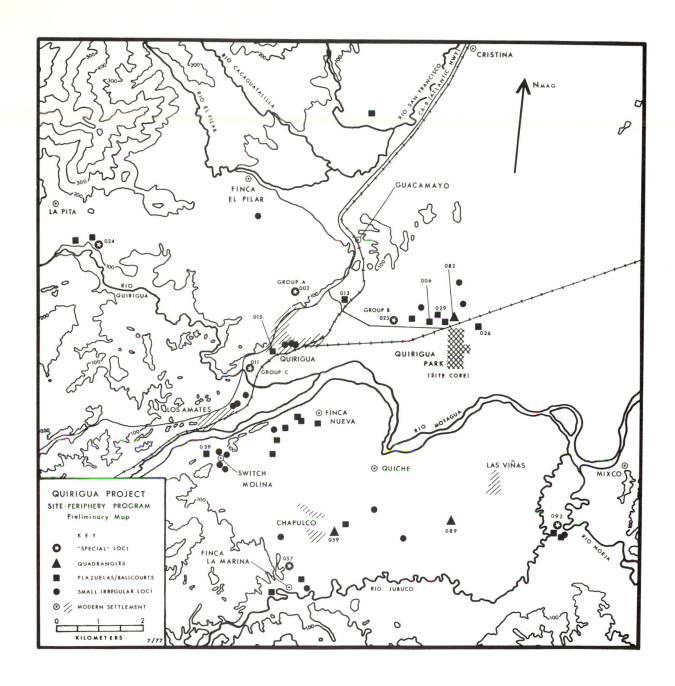

Figure 1. Preliminary map of architectural loci in the Quirigua site-periphery.

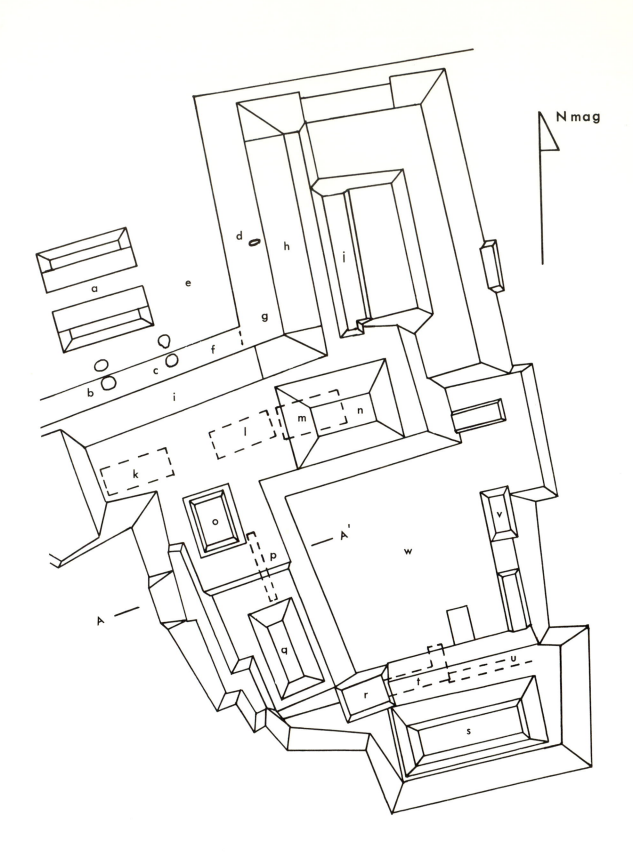

N mag

Figure 2. (opposite page) Quirigua Acropolis, simplified plan view. Scale 1:1000. Broken lines indicate buried structures discovered during excavation.

a. Structure 1B-7	h. Staircase	p. *Kinich Ahau* wall
b. Monuments 16 and 24	i. Staircase	q. Structure 1B-3
c. Monuments 15 and 23	j. Structure 1B-17	r. Structure 1B-2
d. Pedestal stone	k. Structure 1B-Sub.2	s. Structure 1B-1-1st
e. Ballcourt Plaza	l. Structure 1B-Sub.3	t. Structure 1B-1-2nd
f. Terrace	m. Structure 1B-5-2nd	u. Free-standing wall
g. Terrace	n. Structure 1B-5-1st	v. Structure 1B-6
	o. Structure 1B-4	w. Acropolis Plaza

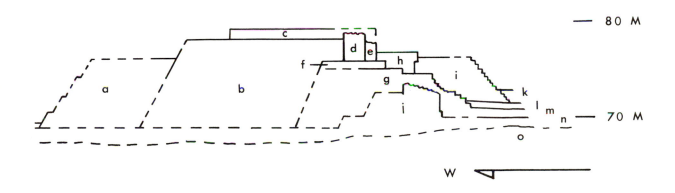

Figure 3. Quirigua Acropolis, schematic east-west section through west side (A-A' of Fig. 2). Scale 1:400.

Pre-construction surface:	o
Early construction:	j
Early western platform:	g, f
Kinich Ahau wall:	d
Expansions into West Court:	a, b
Acropolis Plaza floors:	k, l, m, n
Later western platform:	c, e, h, i

a

b

Figure 4. Quirigua Site-Core, 1976.
   a.   Temporary bracing for Monument 10 after earthquake of February 4, 1976.
   b.   Ballcourt Plaza after clearing, with the east staircase at left. Corner terraces and Str. 1B-5 at right.

a

b

Figure 5. Excavations in the Acropolis, 1976.
    a.   Aerial view of Quirigua Acropolis, from the north. Metal sheets cover *Kinich Ahau* wall and adjacent trench.
    b.   Aerial view of Quirigua Acropolis, from the southeast.

a

b

c

Figure 6. Architecture in the Acropolis.

    a.   Rear (south) wall of Str. 1B-1-2nd running under secondary buttress of Str. 1B-2.

    b.   Central stone mosaic medallion on south (rear) wall of Str. 1B-2.

    c.   Front stair (east side) of Str. 1B-3.

a

b

Figure 7. Architecture in the Acropolis.
   a.   View of Str. 1B-4 from Str. 1B-5.
   b.   North end of buried stairway and flanking terrace wall of early western platform.

71

Figure 8. Magnetometer survey and the Quirigua causeway.
  a. Bruce Bevan (right) conducting magnetic survey at Quirigua.
  b. Bevan testing which specific construction stones were source of magnetic anomaly. Note depth of alluvium overlying construction of causeway feature.
  c. Aerial view of causeway test excavations, northeast of Quirigua site-core. West is at top of photograph.

72

a

b

c

Figure 9. Excavations in the Site-Periphery, 1976.
    a.   Locus 026, Str. 2C-3, view from southwest.
    b.   Locus 026, burial in Str. 2C-3, from the west.
    c.   Locus 029, buried chamber of Str. 3C-2, from the west.

UNIVERSITY MUSEUM MONOGRAPHS

F. R. Steele
*1   THE CODE OF LIPIT-ISTAR.
1949. 28 pp. 7 pls.

S. N. Kramer
*2   SCHOOLDAYS: A SUMERIAN COMPOSITON RELATING TO
THE EDUCATION OF A SCRIBE.
1949. 19 pp. 4 pls.

J. A. Mason
3   THE LANGUAGE OF THE PAPAGO OF ARIZONA.
1950. 84 pp.

A. J. Tobler
*4   EXCAVATIONS AT TEPE GAWRA (Vol. 11).
1950. ii + 260 pp. 182 pls.

C. S. Coon
*5   CAVE EXPLORATIONS IN IRAN 1949.
1951. ii + 125 pp. 33 illus. in text. 15 pls.

J. H. Moss (and others)
*6   EARLY MAN IN THE EDEN VALLEY.
1951. vi + 124 pp. 32 figs. in text. 9 pls

S. N. Kramer
*7   ENMERKAR AND THE LORD OF ARATTA: A SUMERIAN EPIC
TALE OF IRAQ AND IRAN.
1952. iv + 55 pp. 28 pls.

J. L. Giddings, Jr.
*8   THE ARCTIC WOODLAND CULTURE OF THE KOBUK RIVER.
1952. x + 144 pp. 43 figs. in text. 46 pls.

D. H. Cox
9   A THIRD CENTURY HOARD OF TETRADRACHMS FROM
GORDION.
1953. v + 20 pp. 1 map in text. 8 pls.

Ward Goodenough
10   NATIVE ASTRONOMY IN THE CENTRAL CAROLINES.
1953. 46 pp. 4 figs. in text. 1 map.

J. H. and S. H. Young
11   TERRACOTTA FIGURINES FROM KOURION IN CYPRUS.
1955. x + 260 pp. 3 plans. 17 figs. in text. 75 pls.

D. Swindler
12 A STUDY OF THE CRANIAL AND SKELETAL MATERIAL
FROM NIPPUR.
1956. v + 40 pp. 8 pls.

M. J. Mellink
13 A HITTITE CEMETERY AT GORDION.
1956. xii + 60 pp. 30 pls.

Linton Satterthwaite
14 STONE ARTIFACTS AT AND NEAR THE FINLEY SITE, NEAR
EDEN, WYOMING.
1957. iv + 22 pp. 5 figs.

Edwin M. Shook, William R. Coe, and Vivian L. Broman, Linton
Satterthwaite
15 TIKAL REPORTS, NUMBERS 1 - 4.
1958. vi + 150 pp. 26 figs.

Rudolf Anthes (with contributions by Hasan S. K. Bakry, John
Dimick, Henry G. Fischer, Labib Habachi, Jean Jacquet)
16 MIT RAHINEH 1955
1958. vi + 93 pp. 18 figs. in text. 45 pls. Map.

James B. Pritchard
17 HEBREW INSCRIPTIONS AND STAMPS FROM GIBEON.
1959. vi + 32 pp. 12 figs.

William R. Coe
18 PIEDRAS NEGRAS ARCHAEOLOGY: ARTIFACTS, CACHES
AND BURIALS.
1959. x + 245 pp. 69 figs.

Edmund I. Gordon
*19 SUMERIAN PROVERBS: GLIMPSES OF EVERYDAY LIFE IN
ANCIENT MESOPOTAMIA.
1959. xxvi + 556 pp. 79 pls.

Richard E. W. Adams, Vivian L. Broman, William R. Coe,
William A. Haviland, Ruben E. Reina, Linton Satterthwaite,
Edwin M. Shook, Aubrey S. Trik
20 TIKAL REPORTS, NUMBERS 5-10.
1961. iv + 225 pp. 73 pls.

Robert F. Carr and James E. Hazard
21 TIKAL REPORTS, NO. 11.
1961. Portfolio of 10 maps and iv + 24 pp.

James B. Pritchard
22 THE WATER SYSTEM OF GIBEON.
1961. viii + 34 pp. 48 figs.

Porphyrios Dikaois (with contributions by J. Lawrence Angel, M. Stekelis, F. E. Zeuner and A. Grosvenor Ellis, S. P. Dance)
23   SOTIRA.
1961.   xiii + 252 pp.   122 pls.

Daris R. Swindler
24   A RACIAL STUDY OF THE WEST NAKANAI.
1962.   viii + 59 pp.   9 pls.   3 figs.

James B. Pritchard
25   THE BRONZE AGE CEMETERY AT GIBEON.
1963.   x + 123 pp.   100 figs.

James B. Pritchard
26   WINERY, DEFENSES, AND SOUNDINGS AT GIBEON.
1964.   viii + 85 pp.   100 figs.

Rudolf Anthes (with contributions by Ibrahim Abdel Aziz, Hasan S. K. Bakry, Henry G. Fischer, Labib Habachi, Jean Jacquet, William K. Simpson, Jean Yoyotte)
27   MIT RAHINEH 1956.
1965.   x + 170 pp.   21 figs. in text.   69 pls.

Frances James
28   THE IRON AGE AT BETH SHAN.
1966.   xviii + 369 pp.   128 figs.

Froelich G. Rainey and Carlo M. Lerici (with the collaboration of Orville H. Bullitt)
29   THE SEARCH FOR SYBARIS 1960-1965.
1967.   xix + 313 pp.   26 pls.   Map supplement: 8 maps.

Ina VanStan
30   TEXTILES FROM BENEATH THE TEMPLE OF PACHACAMAC, PERU.
1967.   vii + 91 pp.   5 tables.   78 figs.

Carleton S. Coon (in collaboration with Harvey M. Bricker, Frederick Johnson and C. C. Lamberg-Karlovsky)
31   YENGEMA CAVE REPORT.
1968.   77 pp.   35 pls.

J. L. Benson with contributions by Edith Porada and J. Lawrence Angel
32   BAMBOULA AT KOURION.
1972.   xvi + 252 pp.   74 pls.

Eliezer D. Oren
33   THE NORTHERN CEMETERY OF BETH SHAN.
1972.   xx + c. 300 pp.   84 figs.

J. L. Benson with contributions by Edith Porada and E. A. and
H. W. Catling
34 THE NECROPOLIS OF KALORIZIKI. STUDIES IN MEDITERRA-
NEAN ARCHAEOLOGY, VOL. XXXVI.
1973. 202 pp. 63 pls.

James B. Pritchard with contributions by William P. Anderson,
Ellen Herscher and Javier Teixidor
35 SAREPTA: A PRELIMINARY REPORT ON THE IRON AGE.
1975. ix + 114 pp. 63 figs.

Robert J. Sharer, General Editor
36 THE PREHISTORY OF CHALCHUAPA, EL SALVADOR.
1978. 3 vols.
Vol. I: xv + 194 pp. 26 tables. 87 figs. including 8 maps in pocket.
Vol. II: xx + 211 pp. 12 tables. 38 figs.
Vol. III: xvii + 226 pp. 9 tables. 39 figs.

Robert J. Sharer, General Editor; Wendy Ashmore, Volume
Editor
37 QUIRIGUA REPORTS, VOLUME I, PAPERS 1-5
1979. ix + 73 pp. 4 tables. 24 figs. Site map.

John Bockstoce
38 THE ARCHAEOLOGY OF CAPE NOME, ALASKA.
1979. xiv + 133 pp. 3 tables frontispiece 28 figs.
9 pls. 3 maps.
(In press)

Irene J. Winter
39 HASANLU SPECIAL STUDIES, VOLUME I: THE HASANLU
BREASTPLATE.
(In preparation)

Oscar White Muscarella
40 HASANLU SPECIAL STUDIES, VOLUME II: THE HASANLU
IVORIES.
(In preparation)

James B. Pritchard
41 TELL ES-SA'IDIYEH.
(In preparation)

* Out of print.